EQUAL PROTECTION UNDER GOD

Gender Equality and Women's Roles
in the Church

TANYA HALLFORD HENDRIX

ISBN: 978-1-946629-92-0

TABLE OF CONTENTS

ACKNOWLEDGMENTS

A very special thank you to Jeannine Bystricky, who was so kind and generous to volunteer her grammar expertise for the first proofread of my manuscript. She provided invaluable assistance. Thank you to Marsha Malcolm for her editing services. For my friend, Kathy Smith, who generously donated her photography talents for the cover photo and headshot, thank you for lending your incredible talent to my project.

To my dad, William Joseph Hallford (1947-2006), who challenged me to think critically and would have been incredibly proud, but still told me I was wrong. I wish you were here to be part of this. To my mom, Juanita Coleman, who was the one who showed me that there is nothing a woman can't do and that I should fight to be treated equally. She truly embodies the "strength of a woman." I am eternally grateful God chose you as my parents.

To my husband, Ron, you are quite simply amazing. I could write a book about how wonderfully you love me, but words fail me as I try to express how much I love you. Thank you for your support, patience, encouragement, and love.

INTRODUCTION

We the People. Those three words conjure up definitive images and thoughts in the minds of the people of the United States of America. For some, it evokes feelings of patriotism, pride, images of an American flag flapping in the wind, voting, and breathing the air of freedom. In this country, it's the cornerstone to equality; freedom from slavery; liberty from oppression, and to the rights of life, liberty, and the pursuit of happiness. For some, these words ring right and true. For others, the concepts are great, but they have not been realized.

Those first three words represent the standard for which we strive to live in the USA. *We the People.* The Preamble to the Constitution is just one sentence, but contains seven different powerful action statements that could be read like this: "In Order to form a more perfect Union. Establish Justice. Insure domestic Tranquility. Provide for the common defense. Promote the general Welfare. Secure the Blessings of Liberty to ourselves and our Posterity. Do ordain and establish this Constitution for the United States of America."

The Constitution of the United States of America is sometimes revered, sometimes cursed, but we, as Americans, always refer to it and rely on it in our everyday lives. Each time we say, "But that's my right", or "I have a right", we are referencing and invoking this document that has existed for over 200 years. It has been pulled, stretched, examined, and scrutinized every way imaginable to glean the meaning of each and every word within the Constitution and its Bill of Rights.

It is the Constitution that guarantees equal protection under the law, prohibits slavery, grants women the right to vote, allows us to own and carry guns, and gives us the freedom to speak out against our government without retribution. It is the Constitution that prohibits the government from telling us what god to serve, what religion to practice, or where or how we worship.

The ideals of the Constitution are noble. However, we can't always agree on what the words of the Constitution mean, nor can we agree how those words apply to different situations. The Constitution, though expertly written, leaves open to interpretation numerous provisions, how it applies to individual and specific situations, and whether a federal or state law violates someone's Constitutional rights. This document touches almost every aspect of our lives in the United States. In American law, we look to precedent, cases previously decided by the United States Supreme Court and lower courts for guidance on how to interpret the United States Constitution. Although we have over 200 years of case law to reference, we continue to need guidance from the Supreme Court of the United States (SCOTUS) as issues arise in our daily lives.

The concept of "We the People" is also found in the Bible. Paul, who wrote the controversial texts about women that will be explored later, wrote, "There is neither Jew nor Greek, there is neither slave nor free, there is no male and female, for you are all one in Christ Jesus."[1] Paul also wrote, "so we, though many, are one body in Christ, and individually members one of another."[2] Further, in 1 Corinthians 12:12-28, he wrote that we are all members of the one body, the body of Christ.

Both the Bible and the United States Constitution were written by men. However, they were written for the benefit of all people: men and women, young and old, and people of different races. "We the People" does not only mean white men. The precepts apply to men, women, white people, and people of color. And, to be clear, our constitutional rights are not our "God-given rights" as I've heard some people proclaim. We don't have a God-given right to own guns, have a speedy trial, exercise free speech, participate in free assembly, or hold such other rights enumerated in the Bill of Rights of the United States Constitution.

I cherish living in America. I'm proud to be an American. Born and raised in the South, I love my country. More than that, though, I love and cherish being a child of God, a daughter of the King. God has given me more grace than I feel I

---

1   Galatians 3:28 (ESV). Unless otherwise noted, all Biblical citations are from the English Standard Version.

2   Romans 12:5

deserve. My love of country, though, can neither replace my love of God, nor supplant my love of God. I cannot allow pride in being an American to become an idol. The American flag is not an icon to worship. It's merely a symbol of American independence and the freedoms we cherish, not an idol that we worship above God.

But what does the Constitution of the United States have to do with the American church? We, too, look to the Constitution for guidance and protections. American Christians have wed the idea of church and state. We delight in proclaiming this country was founded on Christian principles and the Christian faith. Indeed, the Framers of the Constitution were predominantly of the Christian faith. In the early years of the Republic, Christian church services were held in government buildings in Washington, D.C. Elected officials prayed and invoked God's guidance and direction for their lives and for the country. As a Christian, I believe God guided the Framers in how they structured and wrote the Declaration of Independence and the Constitution.

We often view an attack on American symbols and freedoms as an attack on our faith. We, mostly evangelicals, have blurred the line between worship of God and worship of nation. Leaders in the American church, mostly conservative denominations, have been vocal about United States Supreme Court cases that touch on issues such as abortion, marriage, family, LGBTQ rights, and religious rights and discrimination. The 2016 and 2020 election cycles were explosive. Several nationally known religious leaders in this country spoke openly about the election. Many of those leaders spoke from the pulpit, proclaiming that Christians could not vote for a coalition of folks who were pro-abortion and against the rule of law.[3] One openly laughed and mocked the results showing that Joe Biden, not Donald Trump, had won the 2020 election, insinuating — if not outrightly saying — that God would eventually declare Trump the winner.[4]

During the 2016 and 2020 election cycles, Christians were flooding social media to proclaim the importance of the presidential election on the make-up of the United States Supreme Court. In 2016, there was already a seat open with the untimely death of Justice Antonin Scalia, a conservative on the court. The refrain from Christian conservatives was the seat was too important to allow a Democrat in the White House, so Christians had to vote for the Republican nominee, regardless of who he was. The repeated refrain was that our religious liberties and the right to life were at stake. Liberties ostensibly on the ballot included the right to life, the right to refuse services based on beliefs about homosexuality and the Affordable Care Act's provision that required Christian companies to provide insurance that covered birth control. Thus, the refrain from the same faith leaders in America was: regardless of the character or moral flaws of the Republican nominee, he was the only one

---

3   McArthur, John. "John McArthur Comments on the Election November 6, 2016." *Vimeo*, uploaded by Gracepoint Community Church, 6 Nov. 2016, https://vimeo.com/190474131.

4   Copeland, Kenneth. "Kenneth Copeland Preaches in Lord of Host Church 9am 11/8/2020." *Youtube*, uploaded by SoulProsper, 9 Nov. 2020. https://www.youtube.com/watch?v=ID9XhAXDrhs.

conservative Christians could vote for to guarantee a conservative on the Supreme Court. Only such an individual could protect our religious liberties, right to bear arms, and right to life.

As Christians, we often assert the First Amendment Right to freedom of religion and freedom of expression. This is a right that we hold dear, and we have been very vocal when faced with attempts to silence us in any way. For instance, there has been an uproar over taking prayer out of school and not allowing prayer at school functions such as football games. Another example is the successful lawsuits that prohibited towns and cities from saying "Merry Christmas." We got angry about the protests against Chick-Fil-A because of its founder's views on homosexuality. We have been angry because we perceive these actions as personal attacks against our beliefs and our rights to express those beliefs.

Alabama has a motto, with which you are greeted when you enter Alabama from Georgia on Interstate 20. At the Alabama Welcome Center, visible to visitors is a large stone plaque etched with the state's motto: "We Dare Defend Our Rights." I think of this motto often when I see on television, Twitter, Facebook, or other places Christians speaking up about those perceived infringements upon our rights. When I say "perceived," it's not because I don't believe they are infringements, but because we each view the world around us through our individual and unique lenses of experience, culture, biases, and so forth. Consequently, one Christian may perceive the

Christian baker's refusal to do a wedding cake for a homosexual couple as standing up for his individual right of free expression whereas another Christian could view the baker's refusal to do a wedding cake as a violation of that couple's right to marry and, therefore, a failure to love others as Jesus loved. Paul cautioned in 1 Corinthians 8:1-13 to not assert your rights if your doing so could cause someone to stumble. To what extent do we dare defend our rights if so doing causes people to turn away from Jesus?

What about the rights of women and our place in the Church? A theology for women must be concerned with the whole woman. The whole woman includes our cares and concerns about our government and political systems, economic condition, reproductive health, education, culture, and household. The focus must be on women's equality with men and women rather than being *against* men. A theology for women, and indeed the study of Christ and the application of His life and teachings, must meet the oppressed and marginalized where they are positioned in society and provide them with a liberating discourse that is real and practical. This is where the American case law (jurisprudence) provides help and insight. The cases that have been brought before SCOTUS have dealt with real and practical needs of women such as being the administrator of a child's estate, equal pay with men, being allowed to practice law, being allowed to serve on a jury, equal benefits as men in the U.S. Air Force, and entrance to the best state school for furthering a military career.

If we, as conservative Christians, are eager to look to SCOTUS for protections under the First and Second Amendments to the U.S. Constitution, we cannot ignore the rest of that important document. There are, in addition to these first two, 26 other Amendments that protect various rights and liberties of Americans. If we, as conservative Christians, base our voting decision on gaining the ability to appoint a conservative to the United States Supreme Court (as has been the rallying cry for the last two election cycles), we recognize the importance of that Court's decisions on our lives, our rights, and most importantly, our faith. How can we pick and choose which parts of that important document to apply to our lives? Though there are verses in the Bible — particularly in the New Testament for Christians — we may not like or want to have applied to our lives, the Bible is God's Word. We can study and interpret it and have different interpretations, but we have to take the Bible as a whole: the good and the bad stuff. We would be remiss if we didn't afford that same treatment to the U.S. Constitution. It is, after all, the whole of the U.S. Constitution that gives us our rights that we so proudly proclaim and defend.

In the United States, we have a mandate found in the 14th Amendment to the United States Constitution known as the "Equal Protection Clause." This Amendment became law only after a very bloody and deadly Civil War, being ratified in 1868. This Amendment mandated "We the People" such that the laws of the United States are to be equally applied to all

United States citizens. That is, all citizens are equally protected under the laws of the United States of America. Significant blood was shed and lives lost by soldiers and civilians for "We the People" to have no exception for women, or people of color. Likewise, Jesus shed blood for the freedom of all, with no exception for women or people color. All means all.

CHAPTER 1
STIGMA OF INFERIORITY

"There can be no doubt that our nation has had a long and unfortunate history of sex discrimination. Traditionally, such discrimination was rationalized by an attitude of 'romantic paternalism', which, in practical effect, put women, not on a pedestal, but in a cage."[5]

Having grown up in the church — originally Southern Baptist, then Christian and Missionary Alliance, followed by Wesleyan while in college and law school, Assemblies of God, and a few non-denominational congregations — I saw and heard only men in positions of leadership. Indeed, I was told women were not allowed to attain positions of leadership in the church, nor were women allowed to preach on Sunday mornings. Church and denominational leaders pointed to a verse in Timothy, written by the much-revered Paul, that stated that he did not permit women to "teach or to exercise authority over a man; rather she is to remain quiet." [6]

---

5   *Frontiero v Richardson* 411 US 677, 684 (1973)
6   1 Timothy 2:12

Women were allowed to be song leaders and Sunday School teachers, but they were not awarded a position behind the pulpit delivering a sermon on a Sunday morning. As a child, teen, and then young woman, I saw this pattern in church after church. This was the norm, what I saw week after week, and it is what I internalized. There was no one on the big stage who looked like me. There was no representation for me and other young, impressionable girls looking for something familiar and relatable each and every Sunday. The practice of excluding females was accepted, and I rarely heard it questioned within the church. It created a stigma – a stigma that women were inferior, particularly spiritually inferior to men.

My dad, ordained minister in the Southern Baptist, disapproved of women preachers. If he were still alive, I'm sure we would argue over this point still to this day. My dad and I were so much alike — strong-willed and always right — that we had intense disagreements over various issues. Particularly, after I went off to college and began learning more about the world, seeing things from a different perspective and interacting with people of different ethnic and religious groups, we argued over our increasingly different perspectives and worldviews.

My husband likes to say, "You don't know what you're missing until you learn what you're missing." That was true of me as I was growing up in rural Alabama. I grew up with people who mostly believed as I did, raised in majority conservative communities, where most of the leaders were men.

I'm proud of my upbringing. I have strong values, a blue-collar work ethic, and great appreciation for the hard-working people who live paycheck to paycheck, who toil the earth and work with their hands, who would give you the shirt off their back if you needed it, and who love God and know through Him, all blessings flow. I have nothing but the utmost respect for blue-collar conservative men who have worked hard to provide for their families and shape this nation. My grandfathers, my father-in-law, and my dad were some of those men.

That blue-collar work ethic taught me to dig in, to not be afraid of hard work or learning hard lessons. So, I dug in. One of the most valuable lessons my dad taught me was to never take a verse, or even a book of the Bible, out of context. When I was a teenager, I was reading Revelation and thoroughly confused (which is not unusual for that book). As I often did with religious and Biblical questions, I went to my dad. He did not like discussing Revelation because it is a difficult book to interpret and understand, so he could have been trying to avoid answering my questions, but he dropped some wisdom on me that I ascribe to even today: "The Bible must be read and understood as a whole. You can't take one book out of context much less any individual Scriptures. You must read it and understand it as a whole." As true as it was with understanding Revelation, it's also true with 1 Timothy.

When you read and study the Bible as a whole, you start to see and understand the character of God. With that foundation, read Paul's letters – all of them. When you read the entire Bible and all of Paul's letters, you learn the stigma of inferiority is man-made, not God-made. The stigma created by man has turned many women away from the church and ultimately from God. When a young woman doesn't see her full value in God and God's representatives on earth, she will look elsewhere. We Christians will use the term "world" in a derogatory manner to refer to everything that's not contained in the four walls of the church or revered in the Bible. However, the world can teach us a few things that are in line with God's character. The world, at least within the borders of the United States of America, embraces the idea of women in leadership roles, upholding women with value independent of their spouses and children. Ultimately, the American courts have embraced the idea that women are not inferior to men.

American law recognizes that sex classifications stigmatize when women are excluded from occupations thought to be more appropriate to men. Women were once told they couldn't be lawyers because the court system was too ugly and nasty for women's sensibilities. We women lawyers have shattered that misconception. A 2019 survey concluded that almost 40% of the lawyers in the United States are women.[7] Likewise, women in the church have been told leadership and the pastorate is not suited for their sensibilities of compassion, mercy, and kindness, which make them more vulnerable

---

7   "Legal Services: Share of lawyers by gender U.S. 2019," Statista. https://www.statista.com/statistics/1086790/share-lawyers-united-states-gender/ accessed January 17, 2021

to deception.[8] When women were told they couldn't receive the same military benefits that men received because it was inconceivable that a man would need assistance from a woman, the U.S. Supreme Court intervened and delivered an opinion that stripped away that stigma.[9] When a mother was told she couldn't be the administrator over her son's estate because she was the mom and not the dad, the U.S. Supreme Court again delivered an opinion that dealt a blow to that stigma.[10] When women were told they couldn't meet the standards required for military service and the grueling admission and course requirements at Virginia Military Institute, the U.S. Supreme Court again intervened and stripped away the stigma of inferiority.[11] The United States is fortunate to have recognized the value of women in the military, because we have some truly "badass women" protecting our country.

Early Lesson in Inequality

When I was about eight years old, my older brother played Little League baseball. I was always at the ballpark with him and my parents. I watched all of his practices and games, I raised money for the team, and I cheered them on each and every step of the way – so much so that I was named Team Queen. I loved baseball and wanted to play. My parents told

---

8   McArthur, John. "Does the Bible Permit a Woman to Preach?" *Youtube*, uploaded by Grace to You, 8 Nov. 2019. https://www.youtube.com/watch?v=n8ncOf82ZJ0&feature=emb_logo accessed January 10, 2021.
9   *Frontiero v Richardson* 411 US 677 (1973)
10   *Reed v Reed* 404 US 71 (1971)
11   *U.S. v Virginia Military Institute* 518 US 515 (1996)

me that I couldn't play baseball, but I could play softball with the girls. WHAT?! I didn't want to play softball with the girls, I wanted to play baseball with the boys. At eight years old, I didn't understand equal rights or equal protection; I just understood that the girls had a designated field in a remote part of the ballpark, they used a different ball, and the game seemed to be a daintier version of what I saw my brother play. I refused to play the girls' game. In my eight-year-old eyes and brain, softball seemed inferior to baseball and I didn't want to do something inferior. Why did they have to be separate anyway? I didn't understand it all. All I knew was that if I couldn't play with the boys, I wanted nothing to do with playing ball.

That single decision as an eight-year-old shaped my view of sports and inequality throughout my early and adolescent years. I didn't want to play anything. My dad, as great a man as he was, didn't encourage me to play sports as he did my brother. There weren't as many sports offered to girls in my school and hometown as there were to boys. There just didn't seem an opportunity for girls or even any effort to provide opportunities to girls as it was to boys. This was in the early 1980s, and thankfully times have changed. But, observing this as a child makes an impression that can last a lifetime.

My sense of inequality didn't stop when I was eight years old, nor was it limited to baseball. Having grown up in church and watched announcements about men's groups and women's groups, I was always surprised at the differences in the two groups. I never wanted to be a part of a "women's" group at church. The men were cooking steaks, fishing, playing sports, and doing activities that I considered fun and engaging. The women were having missionary meetings, making crafts, planning bake sales, and doing similar activities that I had no interest in, and, to be honest, I found boring. The few women's meetings I attended consisted of us sitting around tables listening to stories from overseas missionaries and praying for their safety and work. What the women were doing felt inferior to what the men were doing. Why would I want to be a part of something inferior? Why was it inferior? There was a stigma of inferiority attached to the women's group that I wanted no part of. The men's activities were bolder and certainly more engaging. The women's meetings and activities were milder, meeker, and furthered the stereotype that women are to be seen and not heard, that our contributions are insignificant, or of no consequence. It reinforced to me that women played a supporting role in the church. To be sure, there are emerging women's groups that are different, more active, more exciting, but I grew up in the 80s and 90s, and have only witnessed a change in women's groups beginning around 2010 and they are constantly evolving, even today. The stigma I experienced and felt in my teens and early twenties stayed with me through the years and motivated me to action to empower women.

Shared Experiences

It is no secret that men and women think about things differently, have different views on issues, and have different life experiences that shape and influence their views and reactions to everything they do and think. Recently, my mom called to tell me about this device she saw on a social media ad. To share a bit of the backstory, she was an avid — and excellent — deer and turkey hunter when I was a kid. That meant she spent long hours outdoors in the woods. That also meant she had obstacles that the male hunters didn't have when it came to relieving herself in the woods. When deer hunting, it's cold, so you have to wear layers of clothing. This means you have to get through a coat, your outer pants, maybe another layer of pants, the long johns or thermal underwear, and then underwear to finally be able to relieve yourself. And, as a woman, when you have to urinate outside in the woods, it means exposing your rear end to the cold temperatures.

She knows I like being outdoors, fishing, hiking, and hunting. I, like all women, loathe the idea of having to "pee" out in the woods. The device she excitedly told me about is a "female pee cup" or "female urinal" that allows a woman to pee standing up – just like a man! For women who like being outdoors, this is revolutionary!

When I told my husband about it, he grimaced and said, "You don't need that". He elaborated, attempting to justify his response by saying I could just "hug a tree". He didn't understand. He has not had the same experiences I've had as a woman. He doesn't understand all of the processes and fears women have when we have to pee in the woods.

When I shared the information about the device with the ladies at my office, they all immediately got excited, and we started sharing stories of being in the woods and the obstacles of peeing outdoors. We talked about the struggle of having to be sure there was NO one around, checking the surroundings to make sure there was no poison ivy, insects, or snakes. Then, we have to maneuver dropping our pants while holding on to a tree with one hand while we squat, and using the other hand to hold our pants away from the urine stream to make sure they didn't get wet. And, when we squat, we're having to lean back a little bit to keep the stream away from our clothes and shoes. We have to watch and move our shoes around a little bit to keep the pool of pee below us from spreading to our shoes. And then, sometimes it's not a nice and neat stream, but it just gushes out and goes everywhere. Truly, men have it so easy that they do not understand that this is such a major, stressful, anxiety-inducing experience for women.

When we shared our stories, we laughed hard at our similar experiences. We kept interrupting one another to say, "And then…" as we kept piling on the difficulties we've shared, while doubling over in laughter about the stories. Sharing stories like this is not theology, but it highlights how our perspectives — even about a silly female urinal — are so strikingly different.

Women have different needs. A few hours before I wrote this paragraph in November 2020, I watched history being made by Sarah Fuller. Ms. Fuller became the first female to play in a Power 5 conference game as she kicked off for Vanderbilt.

Tears filled my eyes as she lined up with the team for the kick-off, and then they streamed down my face as her foot connected with the football and the ball went exactly where it was supposed to go. My tears and emotions shocked me. I did not anticipate such an emotional reaction to a standard football play. I turned to Twitter and saw that I was not the only woman who reacted that way. Women were posting how they cried when they saw her take the field. Fathers posted how excited their little girls were to see someone who looked like them on the ballfield. Playing football is something we've been told we couldn't do. We watch football every weekend in the fall, sometimes with great intensity, but no one on the field looks like us. We finally saw someone who looked like us, shattering a barrier before our very eyes. Some things just mean more. Girl dads, watching their little girls' reactions, got it and finally understood. We women are capable, but have been denied for far too long, because we are seen as "just a girl."

There are just some things that women "get" because of our similar experiences and struggles. Whether it's laughing over the ridiculousness of having to pee in the woods or watching with emotion as a glass ceiling is shattered, having experiences unique to our sex makes us valuable within society. The United States Supreme Court has recognized that value.

History Is Written by the Victors

There's a phrase we sometimes hear, "History is written by the victors." The first person to utter that phrase is not known, but this reference to war can also be true for theology. Men have dominated theology. The first "Christians" were part of a patriarchal society. As such, men dominated the religious circles. Women were prohibited from formal education for many centuries. Interestingly, Jesus commended a woman for sitting at his feet listening and learning from Him. [12]

Theology is the study of God. The study of God, though, is broad. It includes the study of His nature, how He relates to the world, how people practice their faith in God, and their religious experience. Men have been the predominant theologians throughout the centuries. Men have crafted the way in which we have interpreted scripture for centuries. There were some women in history who studied and wrote about theology, but there were very few. It is only in recent history that women have really embraced this task. When pursuing my Master of Divinity, one of my female professors encouraged me to get my PhD in theology because "there aren't enough women theologians."

White males have been the primary theologians throughout the centuries. And, though we do believe that Scripture is God-breathed, it was breathed through humans and through their social constructs and worldviews. Those with the financial or social ability to study, interpret, and teach God's Word had control over the narrative. They had the power to protect their own self-image, their own interests, and their own worldview. More importantly for women, these white males controlled the

---

12   Luke 10:38-42

cultural narratives. Throughout the centuries, our cultural narratives within the Christian community have been controlled
by white men. In the same way that Ruth Bader Ginsburg
would say the white, male, property-owning Framers were not
fully representative of "We the People," I would say that white
male theologians are not fully representative of the Kingdom
of God.

As an attorney, I was either the prosecutor or criminal
defense attorney in over 75 jury trials. In every trial, after the
prosecution and defense have fully presented their cases and
closing arguments have been made, the Judge gives the jury
instructions relating to the law in question and how to apply
that law to the facts. One of the standard jury instructions
(what was called a Pattern Jury Instruction) that was given in
every single jury trial, was "You may use common sense gained
from your experiences in life in evaluating what you see...."
The law recognizes that we see and evaluate things through
the lenses of our own life experiences and that we should use
that in making critical decisions. That evaluation includes how
we perceive the world through the lenses of our gender or race.
So it is with how we see God.

As a woman, I see things differently than a man. My friends
of color see things differently than I do as a white person. We
each have different experiences through which we filter all we
see, read, do, and hear. It is my belief that God uses those different experiences to expose us to more of Him, more of the
Truths within His Word, and expand those Truths to others

around us. This is not to discount the work of the Holy Spirit, in and through us, when reading and interpreting Scripture. I believe it is the Holy Spirit prompting these connections of our experiences to our interpretation of Scripture.

Yet, the stigma of inferiority has been a cancer in our society and churches for centuries, continuing well into the twentieth and twenty-first centuries. In 1994, the year I graduated from Foley High School in Foley, Alabama, the issue of gender equality in juries, and being struck from a jury pool solely on the basis of gender, was before the U.S. Supreme Court. In *J.E.B. v Alabama*, the Court wrote about this concept, quoting an earlier case, and the need for both sexes to be involved as jurors to bring their shared experiences together.

It is said... that an all male panel drawn from the various groups within a community will be as truly representative as if women were included. The thought is that the factors which tend to influence the action of women are the same as those which influence the action of men— personality, background, economic status—and not sex. Yet it is not enough to say that women when sitting as jurors neither act nor tend to act as a class. Men likewise do not act like a class.... *The truth is that the two sexes are not fungible; a community made up exclusively of one is different from a community composed of both; the subtle interplay of influence one on the other is among the imponderables. To insulate the courtroom from either may not in a given case make an iota of difference. Yet a flavor, a distinct quality is lost if either sex is excluded.* Id., at 193-194, 67 S.Ct., at 264 (footnotes omitted) (italics mine).[13]

SCOTUS recognizes the importance of the male and female viewpoint, *"Yet a flavor, a distinct quality is lost if either sex is excluded."* Those words, quoted in *J.E.B.*, were written in 1946 in the case of *Ballard v United States* by an all-male Supreme Court.[14] Yes, 1946. This is true of not just a jury in Alabama, but about our workplaces, our governing bodies, and our places of worship.

The stigma created through centuries of male dominated theology is slowly fading away as more women read the Bible, study the Bible, study theology, and take their gift of preaching and teaching to the masses. The stigma, though, is stubborn. It took hold of our pulpits with the story of Eve.

---

13   *J.E.B v. Alabama ex rel T.B.*, 511 U.S. 127, 133 (1994)
14   *Ballard v United States* 329 U.S. 187, 194 (1946)

CHAPTER 2
THE WOMAN

"...Sex, like race and national origin, is an immutable characteristic determined solely by the accident of birth..."[15]

Despite King David declaring in Psalm 139:14 that we are "fearfully and wonderfully made", the stigma of inferiority for women dates back to the beginning of creation. The first sin and the fall of humans happen in just six short verses found in Genesis 3. Though the Protestant Bible contains thousands of verses, these six verses changed the course of humanity, separating God from the humans He created and setting humans on a course of destruction of lives, relationships, and the harmony God originally designed for us. It is within these six verses that the first parents disobeyed God's command, sinned, and incurred consequences of their sin for all generations.

It took just six verses to set into motion the divide between the sexes and to cast the blame females would take for the fall. It was "Eve's fault" for eating that fruit. It was "Eve's fault" that sin entered the world, and all of the subsequent consequences.

---

15   *Frontiero v Richardson* 411 U.S. 677 (1973)

It was "the woman". The consequences for Eve and her daughters have been severe.

Eve and the First Sin

We are first introduced to the woman in Genesis 1:26-27, "Let us make man in our image, after our likeness... So God created man in his own image, in the image of God he created him; male and female he created them." In this account, God's command to make man in His image was followed with "let them", plural, be fruitful, fill and subdue the earth, have dominion over the fish, birds, and all living things.[16] Notice, the verse doesn't say that only the man, Adam, is to subdue the earth and have dominion over all living things. God gave man and woman, together, the responsibility. He didn't give those commands for Adam only, but to both. Furthermore, God created them both in His likeness, His image. At the time of creation, God created man and woman as equals.

Genesis 2:21-25 provides the second reference to the woman and provides a second creation story, one specific to her. In verse 18, God states that He will make Adam a helper. The Hebrew word in that verse for "helper," *ezer*, is never used in the Bible to indicate a subordinate.[17] In fact, that same word is used to refer to God's help 17 times.[18] Several of those verses are found in the Psalms, among them: "Our soul waits for the

---

16   Genesis 1:28
17   Clouse, Bonnidell and Robert Clouse, eds. *Women in Ministry: Four Views*. (Downer's Grove: InterVarsity Press 1989), Kindle 2084.
18   Clouse

Lord; He is our *help* and our shield" (33:20); "But I am poor and needy; hasten to me, O God! You are my *help* and my deliverer" (70:5); "O Israel, trust in the Lord! He is their *help* and their shield. O house of Aaron, trust in the Lord! He is their *help* and their shield. You who fear the Lord, trust in the Lord! He is their *help* and their shield" (115:9-11), and "I lift up my eyes to the hills. From where does my *help* come?" (121:1). God uses the same word for "help" in this Genesis verse to indicate the woman's significance in His creation as He uses throughout the Bible to describe the help He provides. Using the same form of the word "help" indicates the value of women and importance of our role in God's Kingdom here on earth.

The woman, Eve, has often been blamed for the fall of man and the introduction of sin into the world. Christians believe there was no sin on earth until Eve took a bite of the forbidden fruit. Further, Christians believe that prior to Eve eating that certain piece of fruit, she and Adam had a close relationship with God and had it "pretty easy." God supplied their every need, so they didn't have to hunt or garden for food; it was all provided. It was paradise, and all they had to do was exist. They ate, walked around naked, and had to populate the earth. The only thing God required of them was to have sex and procreate. And, I think I've just discovered why men are so mad about the first sin. I digress.... It was all great until one fateful day in the Garden of Eden.

The story of Adam and Eve is likely familiar to anyone who has ever been to church. If you grew up in church and went to Sunday School or Vacation Bible School, you probably played with felt cut-outs of Adam, Eve, the Serpent, a Tree, and an apple. However, what happened and what is said is so important, and some of it never even taught, that we need to revisit it.

Genesis 3 relates the story of Eve encountering the Serpent in the Garden of Eden. During that encounter, the Serpent questioned Eve. It asked, "Did God actually say, 'You shall not eat from any tree in the garden'?"[19] Eve responded "… but God said, 'You shall not eat the fruit of the tree that is in the midst of the garden, neither shall you touch it, lest you die.'"[20] Her response was only partially correct. She added, "neither shall you touch it" to God's command given to Adam in Genesis 2:16-17, which says, "You may surely eat of every tree of the garden, but of the tree of the knowledge of good and evil you shall not eat, for in the day that you eat of it you shall surely die." She added to God's Words — His instructions — and did not accurately recite His Words.

The Serpent, with what I imagine to be a sly smile and side glance, assures Eve she won't die. He tells her that if she eats from that tree, she will become knowledgeable like God, prompting her to take fruit from the forbidden tree. After eating some of the fruit, and not dying, she then gives some

---

19   Genesis 3:1 (NIV)
20   Genesis 3:3

to Adam, "who was with her, and he ate."[21] So, Adam stood by and watched this exchange between Eve and the Serpent. He stood silent and readily took the fruit from Eve.

Eve has been blamed throughout time for sin entering the world, "In the words of the ancient sage Sirach, 'From woman sin had its beginning, and because of her we all die' (Sir 25:24)."[22] Adam was the first to blame her. I think the first eye roll in history probably happened when God confronted Adam and Eve for this sin and Adam pointed the finger at Eve, knowing the whole time he had stood by and stood silent with her. I have this image in my head of God asking Adam what happened, Adam pointing at Eve, saying it was all Eve's fault, and Eve standing there with her arms crossed, tapping her foot, and then rolling her eyes saying, "REALLY Adam. I mean, REALLY? You were standing there the WHOLE time and didn't say anything."

Scripture is clear that Eve is the one who conversed with the Serpent and Eve is the one who first took from the prohibited tree. Eve, however, was not alone during this conversation; Adam was "with her." The "You" in verses 1, 3, and 4 are plural, indicating there was more than one subject; that is, Adam and Eve were the subjects of the verbs.[23] If Adam is present, why does the conversation take place between Eve and the serpent and not Adam and the serpent? That is, why is Eve the one targeted and tempted? And, why does Adam remain silent?

---

21 Genesis 3:6
22 Yee, Gale A. *Poor Banished Children of Eve*. Minneapolis: Agsburg Fortress, 2003: 59.
23 Hamilton, Victor P. *Handbook of the Pentateuch*. Second Edition. Grand Rapids: Baker Academics, 2005: 41.

The Deception

One suggestion as to why the Serpent singled Eve out is that Eve was the more susceptible of the two because she did not receive God's command directly from Him.[24] When God gave His command to Adam in Genesis 2:16-17, Eve had not yet been created. It was Adam who presumably told Eve what God said about the one tree in the Garden they were to avoid. Indeed, she had to know something of the prohibition to be able to respond as she did in 3:2-3. Someone told her, but it's not recorded, so it's doubtful that it came straight from God. Rather it was more likely that Adam filled her in on what God had told him about the tree. Because she did not receive the command directly, the serpent's cleverly worded question, "Did God really say, 'You must not eat from any tree in the garden'?", placed Eve in a position of questioning herself, doubting God's Words and doubting His goodness.[25] His twisting of the prohibition to say they couldn't eat of *any tree* made it sound as if God was depriving them of something and portrays God in a negative and cruel way. We don't know what Adam told Eve about God's command. We don't know if he told her verbatim what God said, or if he paraphrased what God said. We do know that when the serpent challenged Eve's understanding of what God said, Adam remained quiet.

---

24   Ibid, 42.
25   Hartley, John E. *Old Testament Survey: The Message, Form and Background of the Old Testament* Edition 2. Edited by William LaSor, David Hubbard and Frederick Bush. Grand Rapids, MI, 1996: 26; Grenz, Stanley. *Theology for the Community of God*. Grand Rapids: Eerdmans Publishing, 1994: 191.

The best con artists are those who mix a little truth in with a lie. Hearing someone tell a story that you know is at least partially true — that is, the story has some facts in it that you know to be true — makes it so believable that you think the rest of the story must also be true as well. It's a very clever technique and quite effective. According to Maria Konnikova, author of *The Confidence Trick*, con artists employ several effective tools such as appealing to and exploiting our emotions; asking us a lot of questions to make us feel good; saying our name and mimicking our body language; revealing their own faults, fears, and desires to appear vulnerable; letting us win; setting a time frame to get us to act quickly, and playing on our desire to avoid embarrassment.[26]

The techniques that cons have been using for centuries began right here in Genesis with the serpent and what he said to Eve and Adam. And again, Adam was with Eve when this conversation took place, but did nothing to correct what Eve or the serpent said. Falling victim to deception is gender-neutral.

The serpent, by beginning his sentence with "For God knows", undermines God and plants a seed of doubt of God's goodness when he refutes the pronouncement that Eve will die if she eats from the Tree. He says "For God knows..." accusingly, sarcastically, to insinuate to Eve and Adam that God's not telling them the truth and withholding something from them. He's appealing to their desire to avoid embarrassment,

---

26   Konnikova, Maria. *The Confidence Game: Why we fall for it... every time.* New York, Penguin Books, 2017.

giving them a chance to "win", and encouraging them to act quickly. Beginning with this phrase again paints God as one who, at a minimum, wishes to withhold something good from Adam and Eve and, at worst, is a cruel god. Instead, he says to Eve that she will be like God if she eats from the tree. The temptation to be independent, to be autonomous, and to know what God knows is far too appealing to Eve, particularly in light of the doubts of God's goodness now firmly planted in her mind. And, there was Adam, who was with her but remained silent. The very person who received the command directly from God remained silent through this exchange, never interjected to correct Eve or the serpent, and never objected to the suggestion that Eve eat of the fruit. Why is that? Why did Adam remain quiet?

When they are confronted by God in Genesis 3:13, Adam points the finger at Eve, and then Eve points the finger at the Serpent and says that the Serpent "deceived" her. The Hebrew word used in this verse for deceive is used elsewhere in the Old Testament. In "every occurrence of this form of the verb, the idea of deception is used within the context of entrapment, i.e., deceiving people into thinking they are safe when destruction (either military or divine judgment) is coming."[27] That is a fitting definition of what happened with Eve. The Serpent convinced her the fruit wouldn't kill her, that she wouldn't die as she believed. The Serpent made her think she was safe

---

27   DeFranza, Megan K. "The Transformation of Deception: Understanding the Portrait of Eve in the *Apocalypse of Abraham*, Chapter 23." *Priscilla Papers* 23, no.2 (Spring 2009), 23.

not only in eating the fruit, but in trusting the Serpent. He sounded like he knew what he was talking about. What he said sounded good to her, she didn't receive God's instructions directly from Him, and Adam, who told her what God had said, didn't speak up to correct the Serpent. So, she felt safe and accepted what he told her. Her acceptance of his deceitful words led to the destruction of the serenity of the Garden and the divide between God and humans.

Blaming Eve

After a brief mention of Eve in Genesis 4, she is not named again until Romans. In fact, neither Eve nor Adam is mentioned again except in genealogical form until Romans 5. This is perplexing given the significance of the Fall. Though sin and the sinfulness of humans are written about extensively in the Old Testament, sin is not mentioned in the context of Eve or Adam. There is no finger pointing or blaming Eve for sin or the ills of society from the end of Genesis until Romans in the New Testament – a time span of some 4,000 years.

The next time we read about Eve, the Apostle Paul wrote, "And Adam was not the one deceived; it was the woman who was deceived and became a sinner."[28] This statement by Paul has been used in many ways through the centuries to place the blame for sin and evil on Eve and, as a consequence, all women. There are many interpretations of this verse, each one used to serve the purpose of the respective interpreter. This is

---

28   1 Timothy 2:14 (NIV)

a prime verse for selective literalism, one that we select to take literally because it advances our position, or as in this case, to perpetuate the notion that Eve is to blame and women are to remain silent. This verse, taken out of context, and without the understanding of the original sin, has perpetuated the notion of spiritual inferiority of women and relieves the man of any responsibility for the fall of man.

During the Protestant Reformation, there was a short-lived departure from the belief that women were cursed because of Eve, but there still existed prejudice against women.[29] Despite the gains in society, they were still not welcome in ministry. In the centuries following the Reformation, witchcraft became a target for persecution. King James wrote a tract about witchcraft in which he declared that women were more susceptible to becoming witches because of "the snares of the Devil as was ever well proved to be true by the Serpent's deceiving of Eve at the beginning."[30]

In the book, *Daughters of the Church*, the authors outline some of the women who forged ahead into ministry throughout the centuries in the face of mighty opposition. Though the book covers the years immediately following Jesus' death and resurrection through present times, I thoroughly enjoyed reading about Pentecostal women such as Lucy Farrar, Florence Crawford, Maria Woodworth-Etter, Aimee Semple McPherson, and many others who came before and

---

29 Tucker, Ruth A. and Walter Liefeld. *Daughters of the Church*. Grand Rapids: Zondervan, 1987. Kindle 172.
30 Ibid, 208.

after them. She wrote about a man, A.B. Simpson, founder of the Christian and Missionary Alliance, of which I was once a member. Simpson was enthusiastic about women in ministry because it meant that more lost souls could be reached and thus fulfill the mission of the church.[31] He also reportedly responded to a minister who criticized his position on women in ministry by saying, "the matter was an issue which God has already settled, not only in His Word, but in His providence, by the seal which He is placing in this very day, in every part of the world, upon the public work of consecrated Christian women... Dear brother, let the Lord manage the women. He can do it better than you...".[32] Unfortunately, his enthusiasm for women leaders and preachers in the church, particularly the Christian and Missionary Alliance, didn't survive in the denomination after his death.

Lynn Cohick and Amy Brown Hughes wrote *Christian Women in the Patristic World*, and told the stories of women who influenced the early church in various ways. Lynn Cohick's book *Women in the World of the Earliest Christians: Illuminating Ancient Ways of Life* offers a look into the lives of the earliest Christian women and how they contributed to this new religion, some of whom were martyred for their faith. The stories of early Christian women, however, are few. The atmosphere of animosity toward women generated by the church and society prevented more women from entering the ministry. The

---

31   Ibid, 287.
32   Tucker, 287.

perpetuation that Eve is to blame for sin is a perpetuation that the woman's role in church and society embodies the divine order of male-female relationships and is used by the church to continue to treat women in a subordinate manner. Paul's first Timothy letter furthers the perpetuation of this narrative.

It doesn't take science or any type of scientific study to know that when someone is repeatedly told something, they begin to believe it. I've worked with a lot of abused women through the years. Domestic violence does not begin with a hit. If a man on a first date hit a woman, she most likely would not entertain the prospect of a second date. Instead, the abuse starts with comments that are degrading, that take hold of the victim's mind to the point she believes them. Comments directed to someone such as, "No one else will want you", "You're damaged goods", "You are stupid", "You're too fat", "You're pathetic" all can take hold into the mind and the victim begins to believe it.

Mind games are also used in sex trafficking. I once worked with a sex trafficking victim who was told daily that she was so ugly she should wear a bag over a head. She fully believed she was horrendously ugly, yet she was a beautiful young woman. We, as women, have been blamed so long for the original sin, told — either directly or indirectly — we were unworthy and spiritually inferior, that we — and the men around us — believed it to be true.

I will acknowledge that Paul got it partially right: Adam was not deceived. Adam's act was a willful disobedience of a direct command from God. Adam was weak. Maybe he was scared as well. At a time in which strength, fortitude, and character were needed, he faltered. Adam remained silent in the face of the confrontation between Eve and the Serpent. He said nothing as the Serpent questioned the character of God and misrepresented God's Words. Women have been labeled as inferior and easily deceived because of this interaction with the Serpent. Those labels remained for centuries. Men, however, have not been labeled for the characteristics displayed by Adam during that same encounter. In fact, not much has been said or written about that. In my 40-plus years on this earth, despite going to church quite regularly, attending various church conferences and conventions, I don't think I've ever heard a single sermon or Bible study focusing on Adam's lack of action in the face of evil.

So, for those men who insist on looking back to the Fall and blaming Eve for being deceived by the serpent, bringing about all of the consequences we've suffered, then I will insist on those men remaining silent in keeping with the man's role at the moment in which the male voice would have been most beneficial and impactful. The hypocrisy must end.

Church history has traditionally taught that women should have subordinate roles. This is based in large part on early interpretations of 1 Timothy 2:14, which has its root in the Genesis Fall story. That Eve was deceived has been used as an excuse to prohibit women from teaching. The prohibition's reasoning is rooted in the deception. The thought is that since the woman was susceptible to the Serpent's deception, she could therefore be susceptible to false teaching.[33] This says nothing of a woman's ability to lead, but rather is based on what is perceived as a woman's innate character flaw. If being easily deceived is a character flaw of women based on Eve's action at the fall, what does Adam's silence and failure to step forward and be a leader say of men's character and ability to lead? This is not to point a finger and say, "Men. Bad." This is to point out the hypocrisy of maintaining a set of beliefs about a gender based on one single action while failing to recognize the lack of action by the other gender and, consequently, not holding that gender to the same standard.

New Testament

It is important to note that Jesus did not adhere to societal views of women. Indeed, the opposition He faced from religious leaders was due in large part to His very public refusal to accept and abide by those traditions. He didn't blame Eve. Jesus refused to condemn the Samaritan woman at the well and He refused to condemn the woman found in an adulterous act.[34] Instead of condemning, He loved with the same love that was shown to Eve by God immediately following her deception. Redemption is found in the grace and mercy of a God who finds value in each one of us, regardless of skin tone or gender.

---

33   Clouse, 889.
34   John 4:16-26, 8:1-11.

"There is neither male nor female"

Paul, the same person who most people believe wrote Timothy, wrote in Galatians, "... there is neither male and female; for you are all one in Christ Jesus."[35] This is true even if we accept the notion that because Adam was created before Eve, men are therefore superior to women, and that the order of creation dictated hierarchy. Such superiority and talk of hierarchy should have changed with Christ, as we are a new creation in Christ. Walter Liefeld asserts, "Even if there were subordination in creation, could we not expect a higher level of relationship in the *new* creation in Christ?"[36] Instead of a hierarchy, when viewing social relationships in light of Christ, there is mutuality: mutual love and mutual service to one another.[37] Jesus died for all. Not for men first and then women, but for all, equally across the board.

That yearning for power, evident in the imposed hierarchal structures in the church, is at the heart of the original sin. Jesus' birth ushered in a new era. His death and resurrection redeemed us from the consequences of sin. The atonement for the sins of the Fall brought about the equality that Adam and Eve enjoyed prior to the Fall, but the heart of the original sin remains in the heart of man; that is the yearning for power. So, while men and women are equal as originally intended, the thirst for power continues to separate us.

---

35   Galatians 3:28 (NKJV)
36   Clouse, 1292.
37   Migliore, Daniel L. *Faith Seeking Understanding: An Introduction to Christian Theology.* Grand Rapids: Eerdmans Publishing, 2004: 147.

Much of the subjugation of women has been based on traditional beliefs about women, beliefs resulting from the Fall. Though it is Paul's statement in 1 Timothy 2:14 and other letters that have caused some of the controversy surrounding women, Paul himself warned against following traditions rather than Christ. Traditions and legalism were targets of Christ's condemnation when He was on earth. Christ did not lay blame on Eve, nor did He shun women. Christ talked to women, healed them, debated with them, taught them, had female followers, was anointed by them, and first appeared to women after His resurrection. If Jesus is willing to engage with these women and allow a change of mind after a confrontation with one, then He doesn't hold Eve and her daughters at fault for the Fall, nor does He condemn them.[38] He treats them as ones who have been created in God's image.[39]

Lydia and Phoebe

It is very interesting that the verses used to subjugate women to an inferior role within the church were written by a man who not only wrote "there is neither male nor female", but who also spoke highly of women and even attended a home church most likely led by a woman. I can't understand why people want to brush aside all of Paul's references to women in ministry and leadership and focus on only the verses that seemingly indicate women should not be in leadership positions in a church.

---

38   Mark 7:24-29.
39   "Let us make man our image... in the image of God he created him; male and female he created them." Genesis 1:26-27

Throughout the New Testament, we read about believers meeting in homes. The general pattern is that the homeowner was also the church leader.[40] With this understanding, we need to look at Lydia, and specifically Acts 16:40 (NIV), "After Paul and Silas came out of the prison, they went to Lydia's house, where they met with the brothers and sisters and encouraged them. Then they left."[41] Don't miss this: Luke wrote "Lydia's house". He wrote a woman's house without reference to her husband or father. It was Lydia's house.

Luke, writing in Acts, does not openly proclaim Lydia was a church leader. Either it didn't need to be expressed because it was common knowledge at the time, or the way he addressed it was a subtle way of acknowledging her as the church leader. Just as Jesus never verbalized the importance of women, His seemingly small actions demonstrated loudly and clearly the honor women held and the importance of women in spreading the Gospel. But here, Luke, with a very brief reference to it being Lydia's home, is acknowledging Lydia — a woman — as a church leader.

Further, the same Paul who wrote those verses about women not speaking in church, is the same Paul who went to Lydia's house. He could have gone to the jailer's home, or any other male's home, but he went to Lydia's. This is significant. He had options, and he chose Lydia. He chose a woman leader.

---

40   Cohick, Lynn. *Women in the World of the Earliest Christians: Illuminating Ancient Ways of Life*. Baker Academic, 2009: Kindle.
41   *NIV Study Bible*. Ed. by Edwin Palmer. Grand Rapids: Zondervan, 2002.

Phoebe is another woman mentioned, this time by Paul in Romans 16. Paul, writing to the church in Rome, instructs the church to welcome Phoebe, "our sister, who is a servant of the church in Cenchrea".[42] This word "servant" is the word for deacon. Paul is here acknowledging a woman as a deacon. Furthermore, Paul's greetings list in Romans 16:3-16 contains 26 people, one third of whom are women.[43] Even to Paul, women were not insignificant or subordinate. If they are important enough to mention in a greeting, they are not inferior.

Celsus, a second century philosopher and opponent of Christianity, condemned Christianity as a "religion of women and slaves."[44] And, I want to say, "Why, yes; yes, it is. Thank you very much." What would spark someone to write that if this new religion were not being dominated and/or led by women and slaves? Women had to be a driving force behind this new religion — of Christianity — to cause a statement such as Celsus' to be written. It's not always what is said that's important, it's sometimes what is not said. Here, as in Jesus' treatment of women, there is not a bold declaration of women's importance, but the references are loud and clear for those who are willing to listen.

Women of the Civil Rights Movement of the 1950s and 1960s will be discussed in a later chapter, but it's instructive that we've seen movements like that one succeed on the backs

---

42   Romans 16:1 (NKJV)
43   NKVJ commentary note.
44   Cohick, 195.

of women while the men – not the women - got the recognition. Therefore, it's not hard to imagine the women as the driving force in the First Century of this new religion called Christianity, but because of patriarchy and social norms, they did not get the recognition.

CHAPTER 3
SEXUAL AND PHYSICAL ABUSE

"But let justice roll down like waters...."[45]

An area within the church that screams the perceived inferiority of women is the treatment of women who have been sexually abused or claimed abuse at the hands of a church or ministry leader. I have spoken to groups of women in church for over 20 years about domestic violence, sexual assault, and human trafficking. It never fails that at least one woman will approach me after such a talk and tell me that she was a victim. Every single time I have spoken. There have been many women over 50 who told me that I'm the only person they've ever told about their physical or sexual abuse. These women have been suppressing these secrets for decades, unable to tell their pastors or anyone within the church, or even close friends or family members. For some, they are unable to disclose abuse because their abuser is a deacon or elder, or holds some other leadership position within the church. Sometimes, the abuser is the pastor or other revered ministry leader.

---

45   Amos 5:24

Abuse of women is nothing new. There are stories dating back to Genesis that have haunted me. I really want to understand them, particularly how it would have been appropriate to allow your daughters to be raped by a mob while protecting male strangers.[46] I mean, seriously? You would offer up your daughter to a mob to be gang-raped and sexually tortured? I have never understood this or why this would have been acceptable. And, why would those stories make it into our sacred readings? What's the purpose of us reading and knowing those stories?

Other stories that have been packaged as romantic do not have romantic beginnings. Though we learn some valuable lessons from them, we need to take a hard look at these women and how their stories can liberate women from feelings of inferiority or shame.

Esther

Esther was a sex slave. Her story has been romanticized through the years, and indeed, many scholars view the Book of Esther as a historical romance novel; but she was a sex slave.[47] She was not in love, she was not loved, she was chosen for sex and forced into a marriage with the king. However, the church, as I've known it, has never talked about her slavery as it did in terms of Joseph's slavery. We don't champion her for

---

46   Genesis 19:8, Judges 19:24. Judges 19:24-26 provides a cruel account of a concubine being gang raped and sexually abused all night long by a mob of men to the point of death after having been given up by an Old Man to save a male guest, a Levite, in the home.
47   Provan, Iain, V. Philips Long, and Tremper Longman III. *A Biblical History of Israel.* Louisville: Westminster John Knox Press, 2003: 296.

fighting through her bondage as we do Joseph. We talk about her being in her position "for such a time as this", but we don't recognize that her position was not her choice, the king was not her savior.

Sex trafficking victims don't stay in their victimization because they like being raped. Domestic violence victims don't stay in their relationships because they like getting hit. I've heard people say that victims would leave if getting beaten was such a big deal. So, "if she's not leaving, it must not be big deal to her, so why should I care?" Well, it is a big deal. It's an assault. These victims don't want this life. However, they have learned how to survive, as did Esther.

Supreme Court Justice Brennan, writing for the plurality in *Frontiero* wrote, "There can be no doubt that our nation has had a long and unfortunate history of sex discrimination. Traditionally, such discrimination was rationalized by an attitude of 'romantic paternalism', which, in practical effect, put women, not on a pedestal, but in a cage."[48] This "romantic paternalism" is at the heart of the glossing over of the reality of Esther's slavery. We've romanticized the story by making her a beautiful queen who should be happy and thankful to live a life of luxury inside a castle with servants and her king, a knight in shining armor. In reality, that was not her life, and that is not the life of domestic violence victims or modern-day sex trafficking victims.

---

48   *Frontiero v Richardson* 411 US 677, 684 (1973)

The failure to recognize this and speak the reality of Esther's story minimizes her pain and struggle and that of other women like her. The story — and the way it's been told in my hearing for my entire lifetime — gives the power and control to the king, not Esther. Yes, she showed tremendous courage going before the king to try to save her people, but she was still subject to his control. She did not try to save herself. She was aware that her predecessor, Queen Vashti, was essentially divorced from the king because she refused his command to appear naked in front of his friends. This command by the king treated Queen Vashti as an object, degrading her and dehumanizing her. Her value to him was for mere sexual pleasure. We can only imagine what may have happened had she actually appeared before the king and his intoxicated friends. I don't think it would have ended with the men merely ogling her, though, and I think that is likely one of the reasons she refused the king's command.

We are only provided with a snapshot of Esther's life after she became queen. We are given the story of her heroics and courage wrapped in a romantic story of a beautiful queen with a crown, jewels, and all the worldly possessions. Contrast her story with that of another historical figure, Joseph, who we celebrate for perseverance and faithfulness while a slave. Joseph's slavery was part of his story, but we do not romanticize what he endured. We call it what it was – slavery. Unlike Esther, he was not sexually assaulted. Ironically, part of his story is refusing the aggressive sexual pursuit of a woman. Esther's ability to survive and endure her slavery is no less worthy of attention and admiration. Esther's experience is not inferior to Joseph's.

Dinah

Dinah is a little-known person in Genesis whose story is very easy to miss. Dinah, the daughter of one of the fathers of Judaism, is raped. The assault takes place after her father, Jacob, is given the name "Israel". She is the only named daughter of Jacob and Leah, the only girl with twelve brothers. Joseph is her half-brother because, though Jacob is their mutual father, Rachel is Joseph's mother.

It's widely believed that young women of the patriarchal times were nothing more than mere property.[49] Wives were counted as part of a man's possessions and listed as part of a man's property in Exodus as something not to covet.[50] A woman's role was in the home, as a wife and mother. To be sure, women were not treated well during the patriarchal times. However, compared to their counterparts in the Ancient Near East, women of the time of the Patriarchs enjoyed a relatively higher quality of life, status, and rights.[51] Of note, women of the Ancient Near East who were raped were punished, whereas the male who committed the rape went free. If the perpetrator of the rape was single, he merely paid a monetary fine. If the perpetrator was married, his "own wife was subsequently

---

49 Fuchs, Lucy. *Women of Destiny.* Staten Island: Alba House, 2000: 39.
50 King, Philip J. and Lawrence E. Stager. *Life in Biblical Israel.* Louisville: Westminster John Knox Press, 2001: 49.
51 Webb, William. *Slaves, Women & Homosexuals: Exploring the Hermeneutics of Cultural Analysis.* Downers Grove: InterVarsity Press, 2001. Kindle 835.

taken out by others and sexually ravished for his crime."[52] The Deuteronomic laws established that if a man raped a virgin, he was required to pay her father a fine and marry her, and was forbidden to divorce her.[53] However, this was not the law at the time of Dinah's rape.

Rape of Dinah

Much has been written about the rape. Some have suggested that it was not a rape as we understand rape in our current times.[54] Some have even implied that when she left her father's home to go into the city, she was "looking for sex."[55] This idea is based in large part on the prohibition of women leaving home alone and without permission during this time in history.[56] In the modern era, how many times have we heard that a rape victim "asked for it" because she was dressed a certain way or in a particular location at a certain time of the night? For the record: no woman "asks" to be raped. Rape is about power and control. A male has the duty and responsibility to not rape a woman. To believe a man just can't help himself is to believe men are impulsive, uncontrollable, acting out of emotion and instinct, and cannot be trusted to handle something as basic as human physiological responses. Such a weakness makes men susceptible to impulsive decisions and sexual influence, and

52   Ibid, 880.
53   Deuteronomy 22:28-29
54   Zlotnick, Helena. *Dinah's Daughters: Gender and Judaism from the Hebrew Bible to Late Antiquity*. Philadelphia: University of Pennsylvania Press, 2002: 37.
55   Richards, Sue Poorman and Lawrence O. Richards. *Women of the Bible: The Life and Times of Every Woman in the Bible*. Nashville: Thomas Nelson, 2003: 50
56   Ide, Arthur Frederick. *Battered & Bruised: all the women of the Old Testament*. Las Colinas: Monument Press, 1993: 281 FN19.

poorly suited for leadership, so I'm certain that's not what men really want as their narrative.

At the historical time of this story, there was also a problem with abduction marriages, another theory that has been proposed.[57] In light of less than clear and convincing evidence that this was anything but rape as we understand it in today's times, that is, a rape by forcible compulsion and/or without her consent, this is written with that understanding.

Dinah, who "went out to see the daughters of the land" was unfortunately the one seen – by Shechem.[58] Without any delay in the sequence of events as set forth in Genesis, he immediately "violated" her. The Hebrew word here is `anah, which means to "afflict, humble, be afflicted... to put down, to depress."[59] Shechem had complete power and control over Dinah. This complete power and control were for more than the time it took to commit the actual rape offense. As victims of rape and sexual violence will attest, the consequences of an assault of that nature last forever. The effects may manifest immediately or later in life. Dinah bore the consequences of someone else's actions for the rest of her life. Having been defiled, she is not eligible to marry in her society.

> She... becomes an object of concealment, the bearer
> of an ironic fate for a woman whose story begins with
> going out in public. Condemned to obscurity, Dinah is
> denied an appropriate suitor, as well as the opportunity

---

57 Zlotnick, 40.
58 Genesis 34:1-2
59 *Blue Letter Bible*, "'anah", http://www.blueletterbible.org/lang/lexicon/lexicon. cfm?Strongs=H6031&t=NASB (accessed July 28, 2012).

to marry and have children. In a culture in which the survival of what is human takes places when women give birth, a childless woman is patently worthless."[60]

She will be forced to remain in her father's home or be cared for by her brothers. What is even worse, though, is the silence. Dinah's voice is not heard and she is not heard from again in this story, and she would not have been heard from in her society. She is sentenced to a life of obscurity. Aside from this story, Dinah is mentioned only one more time and that is as an unmarried and childless woman accompanying her father and brothers to Egypt after the drought, many years later.[61]

Dinah's reaction to the rape is not noted in the Scripture. It is unknown how Jacob heard about the rape. However, it apparently wasn't from Dinah, who was at Shechem's house. Just as she had no control when raped, she has no control over the sequence of events that soon take place. She is living in a man's world and has no voice, with her "fate at every twist of the narrative's journey" determined by men.[62]

The Silence

We have to keep reminding ourselves that the times were different then but, in many ways, they are not. While we now have laws that protect women who have been raped and there are consequences for those who commit sexual violence, women are still silenced. Some families tell their daughters to

---

60   Zlotnick, 48.
61   Richards, 51.
62   Berquist, John. *Reclaiming her Story: The witness of women in the Old Testament.* St. Louis: Chalice Press, 1992: 142.

not say anything because it would bring shame to the family. Some families ask victims, "How could you let that happen?" As one who has prosecuted rape cases, advocated for victims of rape, educated others about rape, and worked with victims in various roles, even in modern times, I am quite familiar with the silent suffering of many rape victims who often remain silent and have no voice, either by choice or otherwise.

An interesting observation made by G. Spivak, as noted in Penner's "Textually Violating Dinah," is that while women are (were) free to talk, "she is only speaking if there is a listener to complete the exchange."[63] Dinah may have spoken, she may have expressed her opinions, but there was no one there to listen to her. A crime against society and against morality had been committed, creating a legal issue. All legal issues in Dinah's day were firmly under the control of men.[64] Even if Dinah had expressed her desire for prosecution or lamented her situation, she had no say in legal matters. Culturally, she was expected to do just as her father or brothers instructed.[65]

This is not too difficult a concept to understand and believe, particularly if you grew up in a conservative church. We spoke up, but we often found that no one was listening.

The silence that is most bothersome is that of her family as to her well-being, both existing and future. The immediate reaction of her father and brothers is that they "were indignant

---

63   Penner, Todd and Lilian Cates. "Textually Violating Dinah: Literary readings, colonizing interpretations, and the pleasure of the text." *The Bible and Critical Theory* 3, no. 3 (2007): 37.1, 37.10.
64   King, 50.
65   Zlotnik, 89.

and very angry, because he had done an outrageous thing in Israel by lying with Jacob's daughter, for such a thing must not be done."[66] The concern does not seem to be with how their daughter and sister is coping, how's she's doing, or about her future. It's all about the disgrace — the shame — in Israel. Not Dinah's shame and disgrace, Israel's. In fact, we don't even know what Dinah was doing during the time that followed the rape. It is not until verse 26, when Hamor and Shechem are dead, that we are told that Dinah is at Shechem's house – and apparently had been there the entire time. If the brothers grieved for their sister, why does it take days to get her home?

Dinah will be forced to live a life as a maiden and child-less – a fate worse than death in those days. She will forever be at the mercy of her brothers and father for her subsistence. She will face scorn and humiliation her entire life. It is the life sentence she has been handed, for which no one seems to care, that screams through the silence for justice. Ironically, for the woman whose name means "justice", there is none.[67] No one asked her about her idea of justice for her rape, what justice would look like to her. No one cared.

There are more victims in this tale who have no voice – the women of Shechem. They become the victims of Simeon and Levi's rage when all of their husbands, fathers, and brothers are killed for the crime of one man. They too have been given a life sentence, for which no one seems to care. For them, there is also no justice and no voice.

---

66   Genesis 34:7.
67   Richards, 50.

This story was written by men, and for men, toward a purpose that benefited men, not women. Though it appears at a glance that the brothers are fighting for their sister's honor, the truth is that they fight because of the disgraceful thing Shechem did against Israel, not Dinah. Her story was manipulated to serve a purpose wholly unrelated to her rape. She is merely an object, her story only a tool used for various reasons, but one of which is to perpetuate the romantic paternalism narrative that men are the protector and defender of their women. The real story — and I think God intended for this to be revealed — is about the silence of Dinah and other women like her who have been victimized and left voiceless. Who will be their voice?

Her pain is of no consequence to any of the men in the story. She was a pawn to achieve their respective goals. Their disregard for her well-being screams through the victim's silence and condemns her to a life of pain and sorrow. When I was a child sex abuse prosecutor, I had to caution parents to not take matters into their own hands because if they did, got arrested, and went to prison for it, their child would blame themselves for that. I would tell them, "You don't want to do any more harm to your child." Tend to the needs of the hurting; leave vengeance to God.

It is the disregard for the well-being of victims of abuse that is so bothersome about the church's centuries-long silence. Church is supposed to be a safe place, yet there are children unable to tell their Sunday School teacher or children's minister the secret of what's happening at home. There are women sitting next to smiling and "amening" men on Sunday morning, who, the night before, beat them, careful to not leave bruises in visible locations. There are pastors, elders, and deacons involved in sex trafficking, sometimes the trafficker, and sometimes the knowing "john." These are issues not being openly talked about. I only know because of the countless victims of trafficking and abuse I've worked with, listened to, and tried to help over the last 20-plus years. In too many cases, the church has become a refuge for the perpetrators, for the abusers, rather than a place of refuge and hope for the victims.

We get uncomfortable talking about sex in church, unless it's to condemn homosexuality. Yet, there are sexual sins happening in the homes of the people sitting in the church and behind the pulpit that need to be addressed. Research has shown that a lot of pastors view porn to the extent that it has become a problem. A 2016 study sponsored by Josh McDowell Ministries showed that 57% of pastors and 64% of youth pastors in America admitted to currently struggling or having struggled with porn.[68] This same study showed that only 8% of pastors believed they should resign for their porn addiction versus the 41% of adult Christians who believe they should resign.

Assuming the majority of those pastors and youth pastors consuming porn are viewing heterosexual porn, how can

---

68   Kinnaman, David. "The Porn Phenomenon." Barna. https://www.barna.com/the-porn-phenomenon/ accessed January 16, 2021.

there be equality within the church when over half of church leadership views images that demean, degrade, and objectify women? And, somehow, only 8% believe they should resign. These pastors, including youth pastors, who are viewing the heterosexual porn need to understand how it devalues women, assigning their worth as a sex object. What could do more to perpetuate the stigma of inferiority than to believe a woman's value is that of a sex doll, to be used in whatever manner a man so desires? How can these men be trusted in positions of leadership over women?

According to the Merriam-Webster dictionary, "inferior" means: (1) of little or less importance, value, or merit (2) (a) of low or lower degree or rank (2)(b) of poor quality (3) situated lower down (4) situated below another and especially another similar superior body ...(5) relating to or being a subscript." Dinah became a subscript in her own story. In her own pain, she was made to be of lesser importance and of little value. Her needs and her wishes were not even considered. Instead, the story became about the men in her family and what they wanted.

Being a subscript to your own story, your own pain, your own victories, and your own triumphs is unconscionable. Victims of abuse are not subscripts. Women are not subscripts. Rape is about power and control. The dismissiveness of the rape of Dinah, the slavery of Esther, the offering of Lot's daughters for gang rape and sexual assault, and the death of the concubine in Judges 19 who was raped and assaulted all night are reminders that the power is in the hands of men, not women.[69] The lack of power adds to the stigma of inferiority. The inability to control your own narrative and to tell your own story furthers the stigma of inferiority.

The #MeToo movement of 2019 entered our conversations, social media feeds, homes, and some sanctuaries across America. Women were encouraged to tell their stories, to speak up about their abuses that they were never able to speak of before. Some churches were open to that; others were not. When we don't recognize and acknowledge the sufferings of others, we keep them oppressed and we fail to provide the hope found only in Jesus and His bride, the church. As Justice Brennan put it, we keep them in a cage.

---

69   Judges 19:22-30

CHAPTER 4
SUBMISSIVE MAJORITY

"'Inherent differences' between men and women, we have come to appreciate, remain cause for celebration, but not for denigration of the members of either sex or for artificial constraints on an individual's opportunity."[70]

S*ubmissive majority.* The two words almost caused me to wreck the first time I heard them in August 2020 while riding down the road, listening to the book *My Own Words*, the autobiography of Ruth Bader Ginsburg.[71] As an attorney, I have the utmost respect for the Justices of the United States Supreme Court. Though I may not always agree with their rulings, I respect their positions on the Court. Little did I know that Justice Ginsburg would pass away only a few weeks after I heard that phrase and while I was writing my own book, the one you are reading now.

Justice Ginsburg was a brilliant woman. She was a wife, mother, lawyer, law professor, advocate, and pioneer. Though

---

70   *Califano v Webster* 430 US 313, 320 (1977)
71   Ginsburg, Ruth Bader, Mary Hartnett, Wendy W. Williams. *My Own Words*. Read by Linda Lavin. Newark: Audible, 2016.

I didn't always agree with her, I still admired her (it is possible, you know). She and Justice Antonin Scalia were often on opposite sides of issues and disagreed heartily over subjects; however, they maintained a close friendship. They did not let their differences get in the way of their friendship, an admirable and enviable trait.

But what drew me to Justice Ginsburg's story was her fight in the 1970s for equality for women. I was interested in learning more about that fight, hence my getting her book. So, as I heard the words "submissive majority" from her autobiography, I had an "aha" moment. I don't recall what she was discussing or any of the details, but those two words seemed to scream at me to be heard above all else. There were finally words to my feelings of being female growing up in church.

The "submissive majority". Those words perfectly summed up how I felt as a Christian woman in a male-led and -dominated Church world. As I looked around me, I saw a lot of women in church, probably the majority of faces were female, yet women were not represented in church leadership.

The United States Supreme Court's decision in *Taylor v Louisiana* noted the importance of having a cross-section of the community on criminal juries.[72] In *Taylor*, the female population of that judicial district was 53% female.[73] The Sixth Amendment to the Constitution guarantees a criminally accused the right to an impartial jury of people from the district in which the crime occurred. A jury guards against any

---

72   *Taylor v Louisiana* 419 U.S. 52 (1975)
73   Ibid, 524

abuse of power by a government prosecuting agent or a judge. The Court in *Taylor* noted the importance to justice, confidence in our justice system, and our democratic system of governance in America that there be more than one segment of society on a jury.

A jury stands between an accused and the accuser. Juries determine whether someone is guilty of a crime, which can result in the condemned losing their freedom. How much more important is it for a cross section of the church to be represented in church leadership? Church leadership makes decisions about the direction of the church which determine the impact that church has on the community at large, but more importantly, how that church will represent Christ to the community and bring people to a knowledge of Christ.

A 2014 Pew Research Center study revealed that 57% of American women attended church at least once per week, but only 43% of men attended service at least once per week.[74] In the same study, 59% of women said religion was very important in their lives versus 47% of men. More importantly though as a Christ-follower, is the number of women in Jesus' life. Though we hear mostly about the 12 disciples who followed Him everywhere, there were also a number of women. Luke brought attention to some of these women when, writing about Jesus traveling from town to town with his disciples, he wrote that Jesus' entourage included, " ... some women who had been healed of evil spirits and infirmities: Mary called

74   "Gender composition by religious group." Pew Research Center. https://www.pewforum.org/religious-landscape-study/gender-composition/ accessed February 10, 2021.

Magdalene..., Joanna the wife of Chuza, ... and Susanna, and many others, who provided for them out of their means."[75] Similarly, Matthew noted that Mary Magdalene as well as "Mary, the mother of James and Joseph and the mother of the sons of Zebedee" (aka Salome) were two of "*many women...* who had followed Jesus from Galilee, ministering to him."[76] These "many women" were present when Jesus died. These many women were loyal, courageous, and dedicated to their Lord. And, since there's not a reference to "many men," I surmise the women were in the majority at the cross.

I have struggled since a teenager growing up in the Bible Belt regarding how I — as a Christ-following woman — should feel and act concerning my desire to be a career woman, particularly an attorney. I was conflicted about whether or not I was doing what God wanted me to do. All the church things around me indicated I was going outside of the church and my faith to pursue a law degree, particularly going to a secular university. I had grown up in conservative churches that honored and valued women as wives and mothers, not as professionals. The church leadership was always male; there was rarely a woman who spoke about anything other than children's ministry or music, and it wasn't until I was in my 30s that I ever saw or knew of a woman really challenging that hierarchy.

Webster defines submit as yielding "to governance or authority... to yield oneself to the authority or will of another;

---

75   Luke 8:1-3
76   Matthew 27:55-56 (italics mine)

to permit oneself to be subjected to something ... to defer to or consent to abide by the opinion or authority of another person."[77] Submission is something that all Christians are to do – we are to submit our lives to Christ. We consent to the authority of Christ over our lives and to church leadership. However, it doesn't mean we can't challenge authority when faced with leaders who abuse power, engage in conduct that is not in line with Jesus' teaching, or deny a spiritually gifted person the opportunity at church leadership merely because she's female.

Back in the 1990s and early 2000s, I didn't know any attorneys in the evangelical churches, but I particularly didn't know any female lawyers in the evangelical churches. Not to say there were not any such women in any church anywhere; I just didn't know them. For the women I was around, though they worked, their primary focus seemed to be family. That was great for them and I admired them for their family focus. However, I wanted a career. My goal in life was not to be a wife and mother, as wonderful and noble as that calling is, my goal was to help abuse victims in the legal system.

I also wanted to have a voice. I wanted the women around me to have a voice. I can still remember a time in 1998, a few months after I graduated from the University of Alabama, but before I could start Law School there. I was volunteering with the youth group at the Elberta Christian and Missionary Alliance. I had been a member of that church since I was

---

77   "Yielding." https://www.merriam-webster.com/dictionary/submitting accessed January 18, 2021.

about 15 or 16 years old. Though the leadership had changed since my teen years, I was still known by pastors, staff, and other congregants. During those several months that I volunteered, I got to know many of the parents and teens and had the opportunity to invest in the lives of these young girls who needed to see someone who looked like them in a leadership position. It was also during that time that the youth pastor resigned, leaving the youth group in the hands of volunteers like me. One of the other volunteers, a male, had his eyes set on seminary, but at that time, remained at his home church taking over the majority of the tasks of a youth pastor. That summer was the National Youth Convention for the Christian & Missionary Alliance held in Salt Lake City, Utah. We had a group of teens who wanted to go. Unfortunately, the male volunteer was too young to be designated leader to take the group to Utah. So, because I was over 21 and willing, I became the leader for that trip.

One day, after church, he and I needed to speak with the senior pastor about an issue. As the three of us were just inside the glass doors of the church, standing in a circle so that we could see and speak to one another, no one else around, I asked the pastor a question. He listened to me and then turned to the male and spoke to him to answer the question. I asked another question. He did the same thing. Not one time during that conversation did he address me directly. It was as if I was non-existent. Here was a man leading a church whose membership was over half female, yet he couldn't talk directly to me.

Over 20 years later, I don't remember his name, but I surely remember how he made me feel that day. I began hearing from woman after woman at that church the same story about how he treated them and acted as if they didn't exist. He had completely alienated the women of the church and they were not happy. It was so blatantly obvious that even my dad — who would never complain about preachers — admitted there was a problem. (That pastor didn't last very much longer at that church.) Now, *that* is a trait that should disqualify someone from leading a church, not an immutable characteristic like being female.

Even years prior to that, when I was a senior in high school and had to decide on college, my church put me under tremendous pressure to attend Toccoa Falls College, a Christian college, rather than my chosen school, the University of Alabama, a secular college. I was forging a path I didn't know how to forge. I didn't know how to be part of a conservative church while wanting to go to a secular college and pursue a path that only "liberal" women pursued. I didn't know how to be pro-life while also being an advocate for abused women and children as an attorney. I was raised in the American Christian church, coming up through the 1980s and 1990s. My early years sitting in the Southern Baptist pews taught me more about what a sin was, rather than what Jesus was for and how to really mirror Jesus' actions. This inner turmoil was real and present. I needed some guidance and help, but instead felt ostracized.

History

Historically, there is a precedent for women to preach and evangelize, particularly in the conservative denominations of today. In the 18th century, evangelicals were focused on converting souls and believed that "All people who had experienced grace were compelled by God to tell others about it. Authority to speak or write was rooted in God's 'warming of the heart' and not in theological education or church approval."[78] However, as evangelical denominations began to seek respectability among other denominations in America, "the free movement of the Holy Spirit was downplayed", resulting in the creation of a hierarchy with men at the top.[79] Why does it require downplaying the Holy Spirit to keep women from leadership roles? Shouldn't that tell you something about keeping women out of leadership roles? If the Holy Spirit is not free to move within a church or denomination, should we want to be associated with that organization?

Though we are all required to submit to one another, to submit to the authority within the church, the focus of submission has been on women.[80] We've heard time and again that women are to submit to their husbands. Paul wrote that in Ephesians. We've debated a lot about submission – what it really means and whether or not women really do have to submit to their husbands. When I reference the submissive majority, it is a reference to women as the majority church

---

78　Machaffie, Barbara Her Story: Women in Christian Tradition. Second Edition. Minneapolis: Augsburg Fortress, 2006. (Kindle Edition) LOC 2120
79　Ibid, LOC2129
80　Ephesians 5:21

attendees and the group most targeted for submission in the church. After a closer look at the women who comprised the "submissive majority" through the centuries, I'm not that upset to be lumped in with those women in Biblical and church history.

What's So Submissive?

Women throughout Biblical history have shown strength and the ability to lead. Though the story of the woman throughout the Bible has not been out front and shouted from the rooftops, we can't mistake quiet for non-existent or submissive.

Deborah

Deborah is the only female judge and the only judge to also be called a prophet.[81] In her role as a prophetess, "she communicates the will of God to her people... predicts the outcome of the battle... and creatively leads the people in celebration through singing a hymn."[82] These roles were traditionally male roles, as they are mostly still today. For a woman to lead in this way and be so effective that the Israelites enjoyed 40 years of peace, is phenomenal and not to be overlooked. Deborah is a leader in her own right — not because of who her husband or her brother or her father was — but because she loved and served God. She was a political leader in her time as well as a military war hero. In fact, the male general whom she called upon to lead them into war refused to go unless she went with

---

81   Judges 4
82   Webb, 95.

him. Interestingly, the true hero of that battle was the woman, Jael, who was the political assassin.[83]

Proverbs 31 Woman

Traditionally, I viewed the Proverbs 31 woman as the ideal wife – the faith-filled, God-loving homemaker who dotes on her husband and children. Mother's Day year after year in church, we hear about the "Proverbs 31 woman: her children shall rise and call her blessed." The association between mothers — and women in their capacity as mothers — and Proverbs 31 cemented in my mind that the Proverbs 31 woman was all about being a wife and mom.

This is to take nothing away from mothers. Mothers have the hardest job on the planet. I'm in awe of mothers who juggle work, spouse, and children. I honestly don't know how some mothers do everything required of them. However, I have learned to view the Proverbs 31 woman in another capacity: as a businesswoman.

She seeks wool and flax – she is preparing, planning, for her family and her craft.

Works with willing hands – she's working, y'all! She's working with her hands, earning her own way, and contributing to her family income.

She rises while it is yet night, and provides food for her household – I can relate to this one, getting up at 3:00 am to prepare

---

83   Judges 4:21

for a trial, to make sure my work is done, all to earn a paycheck to contribute to the household finances.

She considers a field and buys it – she is looking at property AND buys it. Notice it says "she", not she and her husband, just SHE. She bought the property with her own money. Not joint funds, not family funds, not from the husband's check, but her own money. The women who followed Jesus during his time on earth likewise provided for themselves and the ministry.[84] So, the concept of women working and providing for herself and her family is centuries old and approved by God.

She dresses herself with strength, and makes her arms strong – she's not weak! Here, in this chapter we use to put women on a pedestal, one that has been revered as celebrating mothers, we are told that women are strong. Where did the "weaker sex" business come from? God affirms in one of the most famous chapters in the Bible about women that women are not weak, but are indeed strong.

She perceives that her merchandise is profitable – she perceives. She has a good mind. She thinks things through. She understands. Women are capable of using reasoning skills and judging the quality of their work.

What is so striking here is that the same set of verses that we hear every Mother's Day in American churches, is the same set of verses that set forth women in the workplace, women providing for their families, making their own decisions about property, buying property using their own money,

---

84   Luke 8:3

and women as physically strong. In the ancient world — a patriarchal world — the woman is being praised for her hard work, ingenuity, independent finances, and strength. Women have certainly noticed it, but it's not celebrated and displayed from the pulpit for young girls to hear when the pastor talks about women. Young girls need to hear from the male leaders in their homes and churches what God says about women – that it's not just about becoming mothers, but about being strong, smart, businesswomen.

Proverbs 31 shows us that women are capable. Indeed, the Proverbs 31 woman is celebrated for being a businesswoman and leader. She is not praised for an immutable characteristic, but for her many abilities.

Mary, the Mother of Jesus

An evangelist is one who seeks to preach the Gospel of Christ and convert people to Christianity. Mary may have been the first evangelist when she told her aunt that she was expecting a child. She then told others about Jesus' ability to perform miracles when she insisted that Jesus turn water into wine at a wedding.

Mary unhesitatingly obeyed God's call on her life to become Jesus' mother. She heard the Word of God and obeyed, something for which Jesus praises her. Jesus distinguished His mother, and consequently every woman, from being valued as only a mother. When the woman said to Jesus, "blessed is the womb that bore You, and the breasts which nursed You!" she was basically saying blessed is your mother for giving birth to you and feeding you, affirming Mary's value in terms of only her ability to birth a child. Jesus replied, "More than that, blessed are those who hear the word of God and keep it!"[85] Jesus was saying yeah, that's great, but what about the woman of God who did what God told her? She is blessed because she heard God's call on her life and followed it. Her call was to bring forth life, but the premise is true for a call on any woman's life – hear the word of God and keep it.

Women at the Tomb

I am a paw mom. My children have four paws, and I have loved each one of them dearly. Unfortunately, I've had to make the difficult decision to have a few euthanized rather than allow them to suffer through a disease or pain. Each time I had to do that, it ripped out my heart. The decision itself was agonizing, but to be there when my dog took its last breath was truly heart-wrenching. Each time, the veterinarian gave me the option to be present or to simply drop the dog off and let them do it without me being there. I have to admit, not watching something I love so dearly take its last breath was tempting. It would save me the raw and gut-wrenching emotion. When it was time for my shar-pei Yoshi to cross the rainbow bridge, I couldn't leave her. She was loyal to me, loved me, and would never leave my side. I could not, at her last moment on this earth, when she needed my calm and comforting voice and

85   Luke 11:27-28 (NKJV)

my loving touch on her to reassure her it was all okay, turn my back on her. As I ugly cried and sobbed, she looked into my eyes and saw me and my love for her. The last thing she saw as she took her last breath was the face of the one she loved the most and who loved her back.

When Jesus hung on the cross, when He took His last breaths, His disciples were not there. The men who had been with Him day in and day out, the ones who professed their love for Him, were not with Him at the time He needed them most. John is the only disciple to be named as being present at Jesus' death. Instead, it was the women.

The women stood firm in their devotion to Jesus. At the risk of jeers, taunts, physical harm, and further ostracization, the women stood by to watch after Jesus; they were loyal to Him. They stood by to care for Him, support Him, and ensure He didn't die alone. It was the women He last saw and whose love He saw as He took His last breath on earth as a man.

Jesus

Jesus gave value to a woman who followed God's call on her life. For Mary, it was to bear a child. For Mary Magdalene, she was the first to be given the Great Commission ("Go and tell ...")."[86] For the woman at the well, it was to be an evangelist ("The woman then left her waterpot, went her way into the city, and said to the men, 'Come, see a Man... Could this be the

---

86   Matthew 28:10

Christ?' They... and came to Him").[87] For me, it was to become an attorney.

Jesus set the bar for how women were to be treated. In this New Testament, with a new covenant, Jesus didn't silence women, nor did He tolerate the oppression of women. When looking at how Jesus honored women, I don't believe submission was His desire for women.

Jesus shattered the societal gender bias of sexual sins. As there are now, then there were certain sexually moral expectations of women and male church leaders but there was no "guidance and teaching which would enhance self-respect, mutuality and integrity between the sexes...".[88] In the story of the woman caught in adultery, Jesus treats the woman and the men who were accusing her as equals, taking away the men's power, refusing to single her out for a "sexual" sin, and then turning the tables on them, forcing them to recognize their own sins.

When I read the story of the woman caught in adultery in John 8, Jesus demonstrates how He honors women. In the first 11 verses of this chapter, the Pharisees bring to Jesus a woman whom they had caught in the act of adultery. This was a blatant ploy to try to trap Jesus. The law required the woman caught in the act of adultery to be stoned. Furthermore, they could have let her remain where she was found rather than bringing her into a very public place. When presented with her

87   John 4:28-30 (NKJV)
88   Njoroge Nyambura. "Woman, Why are You Weeping?" *Ecumenical Review* 49 (1997): 427-438.

by the Pharisees and asked His opinion on what to do, Jesus bent down.[89] At no point does Scripture reference her sitting down, lying down, or having been thrown down. In fact, in verse 3, it says they "made her stand before the group." Here's this woman, caught in the act of adultery, brought to Jesus, and since she was caught "in the act" I speculate she may have been naked, standing before her accusers. I've seen artistic portrayals of this scene that shows the woman on the ground, but the text here is clear that she remained standing through this entire exchange.

Instead, it is Jesus who lowers Himself before her. She's standing and Jesus bends down. By doing this simple thing, He is showing her honor, He is giving her a place of prominence over Him. Bowing or kneeling before someone is a sign of reverence or submission. This is an astonishing physical action Jesus takes before this woman who is likely naked, definitely distraught, and very afraid that she's about to be stoned to death.

After He scribbles on the ground, He stands to address the Pharisees. Scripture says He "straightened" up – giving an image of him standing straight up, feet planted as in a position of authority and defensive posture. I've addressed many judges and juries and know that a speaker's authority and power position is feet planted and standing straight. This is the posture Jesus took when addressing the Pharisees. It's also a defensive posture, standing between the accusers and the accused.

---

89   John 8:6

While standing in this position of power, He addresses the Pharisees. However, after He does so and challenges the one without sin to throw the first stone, He kneels again. And the woman, she was still standing. Verse 8 says "with the woman still standing there...". The woman was standing this entire time – while Jesus twice knelt before her, she remained standing.

Jesus was willing to kneel and show submission to a woman who needed the love and grace of Christ at that moment. His action shows the value and honor He places on women. Our Savior outwardly expressed, through his physical movements, submission to a member of the submissive majority. Jesus is the liberator of women in the Church. It took nine men on the United States Supreme Court to liberate women in America.

CHAPTER 5
EQUAL PROTECTION
UNDER THE LAW

*"There is neither Jew nor Greek, there is neither slave
nor free, there is no male and female, for you
are all one in Christ Jesus."[90]*

The 1970s was the decade in which gender equality began to gain attention through the United States legal system and, ultimately, Congress. Whatever your thoughts about Justice Ruth Bader Ginsburg's politics, she was a legal champion for gender equality and participated in many of the life-changing cases before the U.S. Supreme Court that opened the door for gender equality.

One of those cases was *Frontiero v Richardson*.[91] During oral arguments before the United States Supreme Court on January 17, 1973, Ms. Ginsburg said, "Sex, like race, is a visible, immutable characteristic bearing no necessary relationship to

---

90   Galatians 3:28
91   *Frontiero v Richardson* 411 U.S. 677 (1973)

ability."[92] The color of one's skin is not indicative of one's abilities, and neither is gender. Likewise for Christians, the color of one's skin is not indicative of one's abilities within the church. And neither is one's gender.

The 14th Amendment

The 14th Amendment to the United States Constitution reads,

All persons born or naturalized in the United States and subject to the jurisdiction thereof are citizens of the United States and of the State wherein they reside. No State shall make or enforce any law which shall abridge the privileges or immunities of citizens of the United States; nor shall any State deprive any person of life, liberty, or property, without due process of law; nor deny to any person within its jurisdiction the equal protection of the laws.

This Amendment is the one lawyers and the courts use to protect citizens from unfair and unequal treatment. Though we don't often hear about the 14th Amendment in the news, this is the truck that drives most cases about equality, whether that be gender or racial equality. Alone, it is a powerful amendment, but it carries other amendments with it to ensure that all Americans are treated equally and are not denied certain rights without due process. The Equal Protection Clause denies states the "power to legislate that different treatment be accorded to

---

92   *"Frontiero v Richardson."* Oyez. Accessed January 2, 2021/ https://www.oyez.org/cases/1972/71-1694

persons placed by a statute into different classes on the basis of criteria wholly unrelated to the objective of that statute."[93]

The Standard

There's an important legal concept that baby law students learn and that's "standard." The standard is the measuring stick; it's what a court has to use when applying facts to the law. For gender cases, a law, or statute, has to show that the gender classification serves an "important governmental objective and must be substantially related to those objectives."[94] That's the standard. That means if a law favors men over women, there's got to be an extremely good reason for it, and that extremely good reason must be directly related to the objective of that law.

Chief Justice Burger, writing for a unanimous Supreme Court in *Reed v Reed*, wrote, "The Equal Protection Clause does... deny to States the power to legislate that different treatment be accorded to persons placed by statute into different classes on the basis of criteria wholly unrelated to the objective of that statute."[95] What the highest court in the land is saying is that there can't be a law that favors one category of person (male) over another category of person (female) simply because that person is male. Knowing the background of the *Reed* case will help to understand this concept.

---

93   *Reed v Reed* 404 US 71, 75 (1971)
94   *Craig v Borden* 429 US 190, 197 (1976)
95   *Reed v Reed* 404 US 71 (1971)

In *Reed*, divorced parents were fighting over who could be the administrator of their deceased child's estate. The mother filed first. The estate was opened, she began performing the duties of the administrator, and it was set for a hearing on the final disposition of any assets. Then, the father decided he wanted to be the administrator of the estate, so he filed a petition for letters of administration. The Probate Court held a hearing on the competing petitions and awarded the father the right to proceed with the administration of the estate because Idaho had a statute that, all things being equal, the father was to have priority in administering an estate over a mother. That is, the male was given priority over a female just because he is male – no other reason.

Imagine that you are the mother. Your 16-year-old son just committed suicide.[96] The court has recently determined that a teenage boy should live with his father, thus transferring custody to the father over your objection. You know what is really best for your child, and living with his father is not best. Then your son uses his father's gun to kill himself.[97] This mother was not trying to be a trailblazer or a feminist; she just wanted to take care of her son the only way she could in the shadow of his death, and this was the only way.

Idaho allowed women to be administrators over estates, but if there was a male also wanting to be the administrator

---

96 Russell, Betsy Z. "Boise attorney Allen Derr honored for landmark gender-equity case." The Spokesman-Review. Accessed January 2, 2021. https://www.spokesman.com/blogs/boise/2011/nov/23/boise-attorney-allen-derr-honored-landmark-gender-equity-case/
97 *"Reed v Reed."* Encyclopedia.com. Accessed January 2, 2021. https://www.encyclopedia.com/law/legal-and-political-magazines/reed-v-reed-1971.

who was of the same status as the female (e.g. parent), the statute required the male to be appointed over the female. Idaho argued this distinction was necessary to eliminate hearings and make things easier administratively.[98] In the court system, when there are competing petitions or some type of contested matter, a judge is supposed to take the time to listen to both sides' arguments, maybe hear some testimony, and then make a decision. That takes time, maybe an hour or two hours, sometimes all day or longer. Consequently, Idaho decided it would simplify things and save some time by automatically awarding, thus eliminating the need for a hearing, to the male the right to administer estates over the females, the father's interests dominant to the mother's.

When this case traveled through the court system, first in their home state of Idaho and then on the United States Supreme Court, it was in the late 1960s and early 1970s. At that time, there had not been a major push for equality for women as the country had just experienced for Black Americans during the Civil Rights movement of the 1960s. Sally Reed wasn't seeking fame, she wasn't trying to launch a movement or cause a seismic change in this country, she was simply a grieving mom fighting for her son.

The United States Supreme Court, in a completely unanimous decision by nine men, declared that a state cannot favor a male over a female for mere convenience or ease. Don't gloss over the fact it was a unanimous decision by men – all nine men

---

98   *Reed v Reed* 404 U.S. 71, 76 (1971)

agreed on this decision, a rarity in SCOTUS history on controversial issues. This issue was of such importance that all nine of them signed onto the opinion. Idaho didn't distinguish based on ability, but merely on gender. Likewise, the few Scripture references that seem to prohibit women from preaching and leading distinguishes based on gender, not ability. There are none that states women aren't capable. During Jesus' lifetime on earth, He never once said women did not have the ability to preach, and indeed, His actions demonstrated otherwise. Those actions are explored later. The few words and Scriptures referenced to deny women as leaders in a church and over men are based on the mere fact of the gender, not the ability.

The Beer Case

Not all gender equality cases of the 1970s had women as the victims of discrimination. In what has been jokingly referred to as the "beer case," SCOTUS determined that a law in Oklahoma discriminated against men.

Oklahoma had a law that males between 18 and 21 could not buy "nonintoxicating 3.2% beer," yet women over 18 could buy it.[99] Mr. Craig filed suit because he couldn't buy the low-alcohol beer that the women his age could buy. Oklahoma claimed the law was necessary because young males tended to have more drunk-driving related traffic accidents, injuries, and arrests than young women, so they argued it was a traffic safety issue.[100]

---

99   *Craig v Boren* 429 US 190, 190 (1976)
100   Ibid, 201

In Craig's equal protection claim, SCOTUS pointed out that the law only prohibits the selling, not drinking, of the alcohol to men 18-21. Oklahoma's claim that the discriminatory law had an important government objective, that is, traffic safety, was not sufficient to overcome the discrimination against men 18-21.[101] Basically, the Court said, "Nice try, but no." Equal treatment of men and women is of such significance that even the trivial matter of buying beer must treat people the same. How much more so for something of Kingdom importance?

Immutable Characteristic

When I listened to Ruth Bader Ginsburg's book, *My Own Words*, I learned a new phrase, "immutable characteristic." That phrase was from the case of *Frontiero v Richardson* in which attorney Ginsburg was involved.[102] When something is "immutable", it cannot be changed. It follows, an immutable characteristic is a characteristic that is unable to or cannot be changed. Gender, traditionally, is such a characteristic. For purposes of a discussion about gender equality in the conservative and evangelical church, I will keep gender as an immutable characteristic.

Lt. Frontiero was an Air Force officer stationed at Maxwell Air Force Base in my home state of Alabama. Her husband was a student at a local university. The military provided certain benefits to married service members; however, the benefits were

---

101   Ibid, 204
102   *Frontiero v Richardson* 411 US 677 (1973)

only available to male service members. The reason behind it being only for males is that, generally, the husband was the primary breadwinner for the family and these subsidies would help attract and keep men. This case was decided in 1973, before the "quiet revolution," as termed by Claudia Goldin, of the late 1970s.[103] Women were in the workforce and married women were increasingly working outside of the home when *Frontiero* was decided. The woman as the primary breadwinner in the early 1970s was rare and almost unheard of. Lt. Frontiero's situation was an oddity for that time.

The *Frontiero* Court wrote, "since sex, like race and national origin, is an immutable characteristic determined solely by the accident of birth, the imposition of special disabilities upon the members of a particular sex because of their sex would seem to violate the basic concept of our system that legal burdens should bear some relationship to *individual responsibility*."[104] (emphasis mine) The Court went on to write, "as a result, statutory distinctions between the sexes often have the effect of invidiously relegating the entire class of females to inferior legal status without regard to actual capabilities of individual members." [105] The United States Supreme Court made a bold stand that simply being female is not a disability and that being female does not make one inferior.

---

103   Jacobs, Elisabeth, Kate Bahn. "Women's History Month: U.S. women's labor force participation." Washington Center for Equitable Growth. Accessed January 2, 2021. https://equitablegrowth.org/womens-history-month-u-s-womens-labor-force-participation/
104   *Frontiero* 686
105   *Frontiero* 686-687

The Value of a Woman

Equal pay for women continues to be a hot topic. In 2019, the United States Women's National Soccer Team filed a gender discrimination lawsuit against the U.S. Soccer Federation for the pay and benefits gap between the women's and men's national soccer teams. Though equal pay has been litigated since at least the 1970s, it remains a problem in the United States.

In 1974, the Court grappled with the issue of men who refused to work for the lower wages paid to women and the corresponding issue that women were prohibited from performing the higher paying night shift work due to state laws prohibiting women working night shifts.[106] Corning Glass Works had female inspectors for their day shift operations. But, when they started overnight operations, two states in which they had factories didn't allow women to work overnight. Men refused to work for the same pay the women received for the day shift operations, so Corning increased the pay for the night shift, while leaving the pay the same for the day shift, meaning the women would be paid less than the men who worked at night doing the same job.

The Court looked to comments of the legislators who debated provisions of the Equal Pay Act applicable to this case. The Court's opinion, written by Justice Thurgood Marshall, quoted one of those legislators, Representative Dwyer, who said, "The objective of equal pay legislation... is not to drag

106 *Corning Glass Works v Brennan Brennan v Corning Glass Works* 417 US 188 (1974)

down men workers to the wage levels of women, but to raise women to the levels enjoyed by men in cases where discrimination is still practiced."[107] Women are not trying to drag men down, rather to be lifted up and paid the same as men for the same work. A woman's value is not less than a man's.

Ruth Wengler died on the job in 1977 in a work-related accident.[108] Her husband, though, was denied death benefits because, at that time in Missouri, a widower was not entitled to death benefits unless he was mentally or physically incapacitated. Conversely, had it been Mr. Wengler who had died in the accident, his wife would have been immediately entitled to the death benefits. The justification for this by the State of Missouri was that the 1925 state law they were following was premised on widows being more in need of immediate help than widowers and there existed a "substantive difference" between men and women that justified the difference in treatment.[109] Essentially, her death was not as valuable as a man's death.

Under this Missouri law, the working woman's benefits at death were less than those of her male counterpart's benefits at death. Can you imagine, Ruth had been working at this job, thinking that if some unfortunate event happened her husband would be taken care of, and then, he was not. It robbed her of her value and contribution to her family. Her time away from her family didn't matter; her very life didn't have value. The

---

107   Ibid, 207
108   *Wengler v Druggists Mutual Insurance* 446 US 142 (1980)
109   Ibid, 151

Supreme Court, quoting another equal pay case, wrote this law creates an assumption, a stigma, "that male workers' earnings are vital to the support of their families, while the earnings of female wage earners do not significantly contribute to their families' support."[110] SCOTUS, once again, stepped up and said, "That's not right." Women have value and add value to their families.

Being a Mom

In an interesting case from 1971, the Supreme Court declined to weigh in on whether a law was unconstitutional, instead sending it back down to the lower courts for the lower courts to develop more facts as to whether the employment practice at issue was reasonably necessary for that particular business.[111] The employment practice in question was an employer's refusal to even accept an application from women with pre-school-age children. They hired women, in general, as long as they didn't have children under five years old. They hired men with young children, but tried not to hire women with young children.

The parties didn't provide enough information about the necessity of such a rule to allow the Supreme Court to decide if there was some reasonable basis for that discrimination. However, Justice Thurgood Marshall, who agreed with sending it back to the lower courts, wrote specially to warn that even by sending it back down to develop the facts further, the Court "has fallen into a trap of assuming that the [Civil Rights] Act

---

110   Ibid, 148
111   *Phillips v Martin Marietta Corp* 400 U.S. 542 (1971)

permits ancient canards about the proper role of women to be a basis for discrimination.... Even characterizations of the proper domestic roles of the sexes were not to serve as predicates for restricting employment opportunity."[112]

Though SCOTUS didn't decide this issue, Justice Marshall gives a compelling argument that women and men are equally responsible for raising children and that neither sex should be limited in employment for the "ancient canards about the proper role" of women in society and in the home. Attorney Ginsburg made those arguments about the importance of men in raising children in the case of *Weinberger v Wiesenfeld* that we'll explore in the next chapter.[113] We add value to our families, society, and places of worship, whether we choose to be a stay-at-home mom or work outside of the home.

---

112   Ibid, 545
113   *Weinberger v Wiesenfeld* 420 US 636 (1975)

CHAPTER 6
SEPARATE BUT EQUAL

"The Framers possessed no monopoly on the ability to trade moral principles for self-interest."[114]

Beth Moore was told to "go home." When a prominent preacher participating in a panel discussion was asked what word came to mind when he heard "Beth Moore", he said, "Go home."[115] He and others on the panel then commenced bashing Mrs. Moore and lamenting about women preaching. The Southern Baptist Convention, of which my father was an ordained minister, has long opposed women as preachers. Women have been allowed to speak to other groups of women, but there is no room for women preaching or being in a pastoral role over men. In the field of equality, doesn't "go home" sound eerily familiar to a directive 65 years ago to a woman to move to the back of the bus?

---

114 Marshall, Thurgood. "The Constitution's Bicentennial: Commemorating the Wrong Document?" *Vanderbilt Law Review* 1337, 1340 (Nov 1987).
115 "John MacArthur told Beth Moore to 'Go Home' For Having the Audacity to Preach the Gospel and Help People." Relevant Magazine. Accessed January 10, 2021. https://www.relevantmagazine.com/current/john-macarthur-told-beth-moore-to-go-home-for-having-the-audacity-to-preach-the-gospel-and-help-people/

There is an old legal concept that describes what church leaders are telling Mrs. Moore and other women: we will give women a platform – *a separate but equal* platform. You do your events for women on your own time, not on Sunday mornings and not from our pulpits on Sunday mornings. We keep the pulpit on Sunday mornings to preach to men, women, and children and we remain at the helm of church leadership. That's the message, and that's what has been happening in many conservative churches. The problem, though, is that the platforms are not equal.

Origins of "Separate but Equal"

The phrase "separate but equal" was coined following the landmark case of *Plessy v Ferguson* in which the United States Supreme Court decided in 1896 that segregated public facilities were constitutional so long as the separate facilities were equal.[116] As a law student, *Plessy* is one of the first cases I studied in the mandatory class Constitutional Law. Because of its importance, I'm sure most law students study this case in their first year of law school, just as I did.

In *Plessy*, the issue was train car accommodations. This was during 1896 when the primary mode of transportation was the train. Louisiana, where Mr. Plessy lived, required there to be separate train cars for whites and people of color. Mr. Plessy was "of mixed descent, in the proportion of seven eights Caucasian

---

116   *Plessy v Ferguson* 163 U.S. 537 (1896)

and one eighth African blood."[117] He boarded the "whites only" train car and was arrested for violating Louisiana's statute requiring separate accommodations for whites and blacks. Mr. Plessy challenged his arrest and the underlying law as unconstitutional based on the 13th and 14th Amendments. The 13th Amendment prohibited slavery and the 14th Amendment guarantees equal protection of the law.

The United States Supreme Court held that there was no problem with the Louisiana law. They determined it didn't conflict with the 13th Amendment because slavery implies bondage and servitude, which wasn't present here, and the mere insinuation that this is "slavery" would be to run "the slavery argument into the ground."[118] The Court then determined that it didn't violate the 14th Amendment because separate treatment of the races didn't imply inferiority; that is, it did not constitute unlawful discrimination. Separate was permissible so long as there was similar, or "equal", accommodations for both races.

Reversal of Plessy v Ferguson

Separate but equal was the law for 58 years, until a girl dad to a little third-grader decided to challenge the requirement that his daughter had to walk seven blocks to catch a bus to the segregated school a mile away, while the white school was just six blocks away from her home. Mr. Brown, on behalf of his daughter, as well as other parents in a similar situation, filed

---

117 *Plessy,* 538
118 *Plessy,* 543

suit to end the segregation of the schools. The 1954 Supreme Court opinion of *Brown v Board of Education* struck down the separate but equal doctrine, writing, "in the field of public education the doctrine of 'separate but equal' has no place, as segregated schools are inherently unequal."[119] This landmark decision by the U.S. Supreme Court is generally well known and marked the beginning of legal successes for the Civil Rights Movement. The attorney for the NAACP that represented the plaintiffs in the *Brown* case was Thurgood Marshall. Mr. Marshall would later become the first black Supreme Court Justice in 1967. Twenty years later, I would attend Thurgood Marshall Middle School in the small town of Evergreen, Alabama, and learn, for the first time, about Justice Marshall.

School equality as the battleground for a breakthrough in the Civil Rights movement and dismantling of the separate but equal doctrine makes the battleground for equal protection for women in the church all the more ironic. Christians have long decried "taking God out of schools". There have been legal battles over prayer in school, prayer at school events, Bible classes in a public school, and who can lead a faith-based student organization on a public school campus. The Courts have provided an example for the church to follow, declaring schools to be the bastion of equality. The United States Congress has passed laws to give equal opportunities to the races and to the sexes in America's public schools. If secular institutions can recognize the value and dignity of providing

---

119   *Brown v Board of Education* 347 US 483, 495 (1954)

equal opportunities to people of all races and sexes, why can't Christian churches do the same? The same institution the conservative church has slammed for taking prayer out of school is leading the way in giving value to an entire people group. The institution that proclaims to follow Jesus, the One who gives us value as believers in Him, and be led by the Holy Spirit, who imparts unto us spiritual gifts and abilities, is allowing a secular institution to lead the way in affirming and giving value to women and our talents and gifts.

If it is inherently unequal in a secular society, in the education of people in the United States of America, how can it not be unequal in God's society where the education of God's people and the salvation of souls is at stake? So, if separate but equal is inherently unequal in secular society – how can they explain the inequality exhibited in our own houses of worship where God is allowed?

Unequal Treatment of Women

In the 1959 case of *Loving v Virginia*, the U.S. Supreme Court had to deal with the issue of interracial marriage.[120] At the time, Virginia outlawed interracial marriage. Richard Loving and Mildred Jeter met, fell in love, and went across state lines to marry. A short time later, back in Virginia, they were awakened in the middle of the night by the local sheriff who arrested them both. Mr. Loving, a white man, was released after only a night in jail and posting bail. However, Mrs. Loving, a black

---

120 *Loving v Virginia* 381 US 1 (1967)

woman, had to spend three nights in jail, and was released only to her father, not Mr. Loving.[121] Mr. Loving was not allowed to post her bail nor pick her up from the jail.

God was often the scapegoat for racial inequality. American slave owners would quote scripture about masters and slaves in an effort to further their grotesque actions. They would point to those verses to argue that God allowed slavery, even sanctioned it, and told slaves how to behave in their servitude. It was God's order of things they said. Except for some extreme views from far-right people, I don't think there are legitimate pastors in America who would argue that chattel slavery is sanctioned by God or that slavery represents the correct order of creation, making a people group inferior on the basis of race. So why is it acceptable to proclaim inferior status to a group of people based on gender?

The *Loving* Court quoted the order from the original trial judge, who wrote: "Almighty God created the races white, black, malay and red, and he placed them on separate continents. And but for the interference with his arrangement, there would be no cause for such marriages. The fact that he separated the races shows that he did not intend for the races to mix."[122] We, as Christians, should recognize that race, an immutable characteristic, is not a hindrance to marrying who we want and having a family. We also should recognize that race is not a hindrance to doing God's work.

---

121 Holland, Brynn. "Mildred and Richard: The Love Story that Changed America." History. Accessed January10, 2021. *https://www.history.com/news/mildred-and-richard-the-love-story-that-changed-america*
122 *Loving*, 3

In the Bible, we have equal protection under God. Paul wrote,

> For in Christ Jesus you are all sons of God, through faith. For as many of you as were baptized into Christ have put on Christ. There is neither Jew nor Greek, there is neither slave nor free, there is no male and female, for you are all one in Christ Jesus. And, if you are Christ's, then you are Abraham's offspring, heirs according to promise.[123]

I have seen tremendous overlap between how the law treated women through the centuries and how I perceive the church has treated women. From my experience through the conservative and evangelical churches, my perception is that a woman's highest honor is to be a wife and mother. While there is absolutely nothing wrong with a woman who wants her highest honor to be a wife and mother, that's not every woman's ideal, and it's not church leaders' prerogative to confine women to that box. There are women who are called to careers and ministries, who have the giftings and talents to excel in those positions, be the hands and feet of Jesus, and further God's Kingdom. Yet, they've been held back by a man-made system.

Women's Sensibilities

In *J.E.B. v Alabama*, a case decided in 1994, the year I graduated high school, the U.S. Supreme Court provided a brief

---

123   Galatians 3:26-29

history lesson in their opinion about excluding women from juries just because they are women:

> In this country, supporters of the exclusion of women from juries tended to couch their objections in terms of the ostensible need to protect women from the ugliness and depravity of trials. Women were thought to be too fragile and virginal to withstand the polluted courtroom atmosphere. See Bailey v. State, 215 Ark. 53, 61, 219 S.W.2d 424, 428 (1949) ("Criminal court trials often involve testimony of the foulest kind, and they sometimes require consideration of indecent conduct, the use of filthy and loathsome words, references to intimate sex relationships, and other elements that would prove humiliating, embarrassing and degrading to a lady"); In re Goodell, 39 Wis. 232, 245-246 (1875) (endorsing statutory ineligibility of women for admission to the bar because "[r]everence for all womanhood would suffer in the public spectacle of women... so engaged"). Bradwell v. State, 16 Wall. 130, 141, 21 L.Ed. 442 (1872) (concurring opinion) ("[T]he civil law, as well as nature herself, has always recognized a wide difference in the respective spheres and destinies of man and woman. Man is, or should be, woman's protector and defender. The natural and proper timidity and delicacy which belongs to the female sex evidently unfits it for many of the occupations of civil life.... The paramount destiny and mission of woman are to fulfil

the noble and benign offices of wife and mother. This is the law of the Creator").[124]

To explain, in *J.E.B.*, the men were struck from the jury during jury selection. In Alabama, a jury is selected by a bringing in about 30 or so potential jurors made up of people from the community based on voter registry, driver's license holders, registered motor vehicle owners, and other lists like utility customers and payers of property tax. When that group of people, called a "jury panel", comes into the courtroom, the judge makes a long speech and asks some general questions intended to clear out some potential jurors who don't meet the minimum qualifications to be a juror. The attorneys then get a chance to ask more probing questions, some general, some more specific to the case. After the attorneys ask questions, the jurors generally leave the courtroom, and the attorneys begin to decide who they want to strike from the jury panel to get to the required 12 jurors.

This process begins with the attorneys at their respective tables, huddled together, whispering about jurors' answers to questions, the way jurors smiled or didn't smile at them or the other side, the body language, and some general assumptions about them based on their jobs and family. For example, if a panel member has a brother in the state penitentiary, a prosecutor may not want them on the jury, fearing they will be more likely to side with the criminal defendant. Or, if a panel member's brother is a law enforcement officer, a criminal defense

---

124   *J.E.B*, 132-133

attorney is likely to strike that person because they will tend to believe or side with law enforcement. Having tried about 75 jury trials in my career, this is a process I know well.

Unfortunately, those general assumptions invaded and colored the process when it came to gender and race. Prosecutors would often strike black jury panel members simply because of their race when the criminal defendant was black, believing that a black juror would be more sympathetic to a black defendant. This was the pattern and practice of many until a U.S. Supreme Court case declared it to be unconstitutional in 1986.[125] In *J.E.B.*, the prosecutors for the State of Alabama struck males because the case was about a man's failure to pay child support. They reasoned that men may be more sympathetic to a male when determining the paternity of a child born out of wedlock and the subsequent requirement to pay child support and the female would be more sympathetic to a single mother needing financial assistance.[126] It had nothing to do with whether or not the potential juror could be fair and impartial — which is the requirement for serving on a jury — it had to do with his gender only. Assumptions were made based on gender, not ability. Gender equality goes both ways, it can be that men shouldn't be impermissibly struck from a jury simply because they are men, just as women shouldn't be struck based on their gender. Disqualification to serve on a jury cannot be based on an immutable characteristic such as race or gender.

125   *Batson v Kentucky* 476 US 79 (1986)
126   *J.E.B.*, 138

This is important to note because our legal system is a reflection of our society. Most of the jurors who showed up for jury duty were members or regular attenders of local churches and "God-fearing" people. Our judges, at least in Alabama, are proud of their church affiliations and you will often see a reference to the church they attend in their court bios. Courtroom staff and attorneys who come into the courtroom are people from the community who bring in their experiences, their beliefs, and their biases. Often, our churches reflect the society and community in which they are based more than the Jesus whom they proclaim.

The *Frontiero* Court addressed history's place for women:

Indeed, this paternalistic attitude became so firmly rooted in our national consciousness that, 100 years ago, a distinguished Member of this Court was able to proclaim:

'Man is, or should be, women's protector and defender. The natural and proper timidity and delicacy which belongs to the female sex evidently unfits it for many of the occupations of civil life. The constitution of the family organization, which is founded in the divine ordinance, as well as in the nature of things, indicates the domestic sphere as that which properly belongs to the domain and functions of womanhood. The harmony, not to say identity, of interests and views which belong, or should belong, to the family institution is repugnant to the idea of a woman adopting a distinct and independent career from that of her husband.... The paramount destiny and mission of woman are to fulfil the noble and benign offices of wife and mother. This is the law of the Creator.' Bradwell v. State of Illinois, 16 Wall. 130, 141, 21 L.Ed.2d 442 (1873) (Bradley, J., concurring).

As a result of notions such as these, our statute books gradually became laden with gross, stereotyped distinctions between the sexes and, indeed, throughout much of the 19th century the position of women in our society was, in many respects, comparable to that of blacks under the pre-Civil War slave codes. Neither slaves nor women could hold office, serve on juries, or bring suit in their own names, and married women traditionally were denied the legal capacity to hold or convey property or to serve as legal guardians of their own children.... And although blacks were guaranteed the right to vote in 1870, women were denied even that right—which is itself 'preservative of other basic civil and political rights' until adoption of the Nineteenth Amendment half a century later.[127]

Those words about men being the protectors of women were echoed in 2019 when a prominent preacher on or about November 3, delivered a sermon titled "Does the Bible Permit a Woman to Preach?" wherein he said that when women take over a culture, that the men become weak, they get conquered,

---

127   *Frontiero*, 684-685

and women can "sit there with all your jewelry and junk. You've been conquered, because you overpowered your protector."[128] This is not rooted in the Bible. Man is not my protector, God is. Adam didn't protect Eve. Abraham didn't protect Sarah – he was willing to let her become a sex slave to another man. Jacob didn't protect Dinah. Deborah wasn't protected by any man. Esther wasn't protected by Mordecai.

Christian conservative women are not looking to be viewed as bra-burning, shouting feminists. But we do want recognition that women and men are equal under God and should be treated as such within the walls of the places in which we worship.

---

128   MacArthur, John. "Does the Bible Permit a Woman to Preach?" *Youtube*, uploaded by Grace to You, 8 Nov. 2019. https://www.youtube. com/watch?v=n8ncOf82ZJ0&feature=emb_logo accessed January 10, 2021.

CHAPTER 7
FEMINISM

"Blessed is she who believed that there would be a fulfillment of what was spoken to her from the Lord."[129]

The mere word "feminist" or "feminism" is repulsive to many people in the conservative, evangelical church. It's repulsive to many in the South, whether men or women. The caricature of a feminist is an angry, plain-looking woman, with no makeup, dressed plainly, and yelling into a bullhorn. This is the image with which I grew up, the image perpetuated by those around me both in and out of church. The message was clear: you didn't want to be labeled a "feminist." To quote a friend's very Southern mother, "A lady doesn't leave the house without earrings in her ears and lipstick on her lips." The feminist caricature was the very opposite of the Southern lady.

At its most basic, the term feminism means the "belief that men and women should have equal rights and opportunities" or more fully stated, "the theory of the political, economic,

---

129   Luke 1:45

and social equality of the sexes."[130] As the feminist movement in the West took shape, it was guided and directed by white women of certain education and socio-economic class, pursuing a political and ideological agenda consistent with the ideals from their race, class, and education.[131] This view of feminism, inclusive of all three "waves" of the feminist movement, has disenfranchised many blacks and poor, and I would add a large segment of Christian women.[132] Though these disenfranchised groups may, and often do, support feminist ideals, they are reluctant to identify as feminists because of the caricature and negative connotations.

The pursuit of the agenda as set forth by those women tainted the movement and thus the word "feminist" to give the perception that to be a feminist is to be man-hating and angry.[133] In a study of a small sampling of women on their way to a reproductive rights rally, a researcher found within that group fewer women in Generation X than Baby Boomers who self-identified as feminists and even fewer were active as feminists, though Generation Xers were politically active overall.[134] This study, though small, sheds light on the perception of "feminists" such that even those attending a perceived "woman's rights" rally are reluctant to self-identify as feminist.

---

130   "Feminism" http://www.merriam-webster.com/dictionary/feminism accessed November 30, 2013.

131   Rouse, Carolyn Moxley. *Engaged Surrender: African American Women and Islam*. Berkeley: University of California Press, 2004.

132   Boisnier, Alicia. "Race and Women's Identity Development: Distinguishing Between Feminism and Womanism Among Black and White Women" *Sex Roles* 49, nos. 5/6 (September 2003): 212.

133   Duncan, Lauren E. "Women's Relationship to Feminism: Effects of Generation and Feminists Self-Labeling." *Psychology of Women Quarterly*, 34 (2010): 500.

134   Ibid, 505.

We want the equality between the sexes, we *need* there to be equality, but we don't want to be placed in a box.

Though I have a lot of respect for Ruth Bader Ginsburg, where I depart from her, the National Organization of Women, and many others promoting gender equality and labeled as "feminist" is the issue of abortion. Though many of my ideals are in line with a lot of feminist ideology, I am pro-life and that doesn't align with groups such as the National Organization of Women. While I am forever thankful for those pioneering women who marched and protested, I cannot align myself with a group that is so incredibly vocal about abortion rights and intolerant of those of us who are pro-life. I am not alone in this. Several women I know have faced the same dilemma. So, to be labeled a "feminist" would have put me in the same box as those who advocated for abortion, something I could not do. Pro-life women are ostracized and condemned for being pro-life; it's a mark against us and our feminist ideals. The deep division between pro-life and pro-choice women is a limitation to the equality sought by all women.

Being pro-life is about more than saving unborn children. Pro-life women care about the women who carry these children and care about the families and circumstances that give rise to unplanned pregnancies. We want to see these mothers succeed in life, not just give birth to this child and then we forget about her. That's why many of us support, either directly or indirectly, women who have chosen life for their children by assisting with baby items, employment, counseling, places to stay, and other services and agencies that provide such services. We need to cut through the chatter and noise on news shows and understand and appreciate what pro-life women can bring to the table in the pursuit of gender equality.

Jesus as Feminist

At the root of feminism is the fundamental principle that men and women should be treated equally. With that understanding, we need to take a look at Jesus. As Christians, Jesus is our example. We can read the words of Paul and other New Testament authors, but we need to see Jesus' example. What did He teach us, not just through what He said, but by what He did?

Gender studies of the 1970s made the assumption "that in every society women are considered inferior."[135] This assumption is accurate for Jesus' day, when He lived His life on this earth. In both Roman and Jewish society, women were treated as if they were inferior to men. Understanding the historical setting, I look at Jesus' actions and believe Him to be a feminist. Some scholars argue that to apply this assumption to Jewish society and hold Jesus to be a feminist within that society, is anti-Judaic, even anti-Semitic.[136] We can view His actions based on what we do know and what we read from the Bible and collateral sources. In doing so, we must remember

135   Rouse, Carolyn Moxley. *Engaged Surrender: African American Women and Islam.* Berkeley: University of California Press, 2004: 1,2.
136   Jackson, Glenna. "Jesus as First-Century Feminist: Christian Anti-Judaism?" *Feminist Theology: the Journal of the Britain & Ireland School of Feminist Theology,* 19 (September 1998): 97.

that Jesus was Jewish, the people who wrote the Gospels were Jewish, and the first century converts were primarily Jewish. It is not the intent of this writer to treat Jews negatively or cast them in a bad light. This recounts the actions of a Jew toward Jewish and Gentile women. I in no way am disparaging the historical Jewish society.

Reclaiming Feminism

In determining Jesus to be feminist, we must first define the term. Leonard Swidler defines a feminist as "a person who is in favor of, and promotes, the equality of women with men, who advocates and practices treating women primarily as human persons (as men are so treated) and willingly contravenes social customs in so acting."[137] Katherine Sakenfeld broadens that definition: "A feminist, broadly speaking, is one who seeks justice and equality for all people and who is especially concerned for the fate of women – all women – in the midst of all people. Such a definition means that issues pertinent to racism, classism, and ecology, as well as peace-making are part of the purview of feminism."[138]

Finally, Letty Russell defines feminism thus:

Feminism is advocacy of women. It is not, therefore, *against* men, but only *for* the needs of women.... It represents a search for liberation from all forms of dehumanization on the part of those who advocate

---

137 Swidler, Leonard J. *Jesus Was a Feminist: What the Gospels Reveal about His Revolutionary Perspective.* Lanham: Sheed & Ward, 2007: 17.

138 Gench, Frances Taylor. *Back to the Well: Women's Encounters with Jesus in the Gospels.* Louisville: Westminster John Knox Press, 2004: xi.

full human personhood for all.... This means that men can also be feminists if they are willing to advocate for women.[139]

A feminist, therefore, is one who advocates for the equality, justice, liberation, and full personhood of all people, but particularly as such advocacy pertains to women, with advocacy including words, actions, and failing to act if to act promotes or advances oppression. Feminism is not against any gender, race, or ethnicity. Feminism is not against men. It's not "us v them" or even "us or them." That is a lie to keep us divided. Men and women have much more in common than we have differences, most important of which is the fact that we are all children of God.

Feminist theory necessarily consists of diverse perspectives in feminism.[140] I use the term "necessarily" because women are diverse in every imaginable way. There cannot be a universal approach to feminist and feminist theology; rather, a feminist theology "must emerge out of particular experiences of the oppressed people of God."[141] These experiences vary depending on a "social location" that "involves gender, ethnicity, race, national, international, class and health status... family, church and university."[142] Feminist theology must be concerned with women's liberation in every aspect of her life – "political, economic, reproductive, sexual, educational, cultural and

---

139   Ibid, xi.
140   Grant, Jacquelyn. *White Women's Christ and Black Women's Jesus.* Atlanta: Scholars Press, 1989: 37.
141   Ibid, 10.
142   Dube, Musa W. "Who Do You Say That I Am?" *Feminist Theology*, 15, no. 3 (2007): 347.

household."[143] This is where the Supreme Court gets it right; it has shown concern for liberating women in every aspect of our lives. Even though I oppose abortion, the Court made the decision based on giving value to women and our ability to make our own choices.

In America, the term feminist has been co-opted by the more liberal, left-of-the-political-spectrum women. But true feminism is open to all. Indeed, to tell a segment of women who are conservative and pro-life that they can't be feminist is to contradict true equality of all women.

Jesus' approach to feminism was very personal.[144] He didn't make speeches or hold rallies; rather it was in His attitude and His actions toward women and the lessons within lessons that He demonstrated feminism. "Feminism, however, not only concerns the recognition of achievements but advocacy as well. This advocacy means that the liberation of women is a precondition for the realization of the equality among human beings which women seek."[145]

With the popularity of social media, we all have platforms to effect change, but tweets and posts alone do nothing. For example, when I was in the thick of the battle against sex trafficking, walking the streets and doing online monitoring for victims, talking to victims daily, and offering help out of "the life," I grew so weary of the tweets and posts of red x's on hands and tweets and posts about stopping it. Sure, it helped raise

---

143   Grant, 40.
144   Swidler, 189.
145   Grant, 37.

some awareness – but we needed help. We needed boots on the ground, financial support, law enforcement training, and buy-in. We needed safe houses for victims that could become long-term housing, that could also provide a space for education, job training, counseling, and other such services. When I sat with a young woman who was bleeding out because of her abuse, and didn't know whether she would live, the last thing I wanted to see was mere platitudes about "End it." A tweet, "like", or hashtag does not bring about change. Merely pointing out the problem doesn't affect change.

Advocacy comes in different forms, with some demanding speeches and rallies, while others advocate in subtle but effective ways. Liberation can be achieved through subtle actions and words, liberating the recipient of those words or actions and thereby revealing a liberating message to all women. Advocating for gender equality doesn't require you to hold signs and march. Advocacy can be putting in a female kicker in a SEC and NCAA Power 5 football game; having a female referee at the Super Bowl; using your national platform to bring in women to preach from the pulpit; filing suit to be allowed to be the executor of your son's estate when the law said the dad was given priority; filing suit to receive equal pay with men; and sitting on the side of a well talking with a woman about God.

CHAPTER 8
JESUS

"So if the Son sets you free, you will be free indeed."[146]

To quote Susannah Heschel, "Jesus… unsettles… our understanding of the 'boundaries' between Judaism and Christianity."[147] Jesus didn't behave as other men of His time behaved toward women. His habits of eating with the "poor and unclean"; raising the dead; rejecting traditional views of family; showing passion and concern for women and other people who were scorned, rejected, and marginalized, all while being a male teacher and leader challenge our ability to place Him in a box and indeed prevents us from doing so.[148]

Jesus was born into an occupied country. There was "political exploitation at the national and international level. Social rootlessness and homelessness also became common."[149] Jesus, throughout His ministry, demonstrated through His words and actions solidarity with those in His society who were poor,

---

146   John 8:36
147   Jackson, 98.
148   Alliaume, Karen Trimbe. "The Risks of Repeating Ourselves: Reading Feminist/Womanist Figures of Jesus." *CrossCurrents* 42, no. 2 (1998): 198-218.
149   Dube, 348.

outcast, scorned, marginalized, abused, mistreated, and homeless. He and His disciples left their jobs and homes, often living among the outcasts — the oppressed — to preach and teach.[150] With Jesus, the Word truly became flesh.

In particular, women were treated as inferior during that time. Women were not allowed to: read Scriptures, recite morning prayers or prayers at meals, be counted toward a quorum, come within the inner portion of the great temple, or initiate a divorce.[151] Additionally, women were not considered reliable; they could not bear legal witness.[152] Their word wasn't sufficient or trusted. As will be discussed later, Jesus turned all of this on its head.

Some scholars refute that Jesus was a feminist or women's liberator. Some view the stories of how Jesus assisted women as furthering the tale of the heroic male coming to the aid of the damsel in distress.[153] Well, in a way, He was. Women can't achieve equality alone. We need men to step up and help us. Jesus was the hero coming to the aid of men and women.

There are those who believe that Jesus' mere maleness prevents Him from being a liberator.[154] Hogwash. It is that type of ultra-feminist approach that disenfranchises many women, such as myself. It is that type of approach that hinders the growth of feminism within the church. In rebuttal, Letty

---

150   Ibid, 348.
151   Swidler, 18-20.
152   Swidler, 24.
153   Fuchs, Esther. "Moses/Jesus/Women: Does The New Testament Offer a Feminist Message?" *CrossCurrents* (Winter 1999-2000): 472.
154   Wainwright, Elaine M. *Shall We Look for Another?* Maryknoll: Orbis Books, 1998: 10.

Russell and others state that the "maleness of Jesus is totally irrelevant... 'to think of Christ first in terms of His male sex or His racial origin is to revert again to a biological determinism which affirms that the most important thing about a person is his or her sex or colour.'"[155] This is the very thing we are fighting against. For feminists to focus on His maleness is to do the very thing they complain about being done to women. Indeed, liberal icon the Notorious R.B.G. fought against that very idea.

Attorney Ruth Bader Ginsburg's earliest success in gender equality cases came when she represented male plaintiffs arguing they – the men – were discriminated against. The case of *Weinberger v Wiesenfeld* hinged on whether men were discriminated against by the Social Security Administration.[156] In this case, Mr. Wiesenfeld's wife died in childbirth, leaving him to care for an infant. He applied for social security benefits that would allow him to remain home to care for the newborn, but they were denied because at the time, death benefits were only available to women whose husbands had died; there was no provision for husbands who had been widowed. Ruth Bader Ginsburg was Mr. Wiesenfeld's lawyer and the one who argued it before SCOTUS. In a unanimous opinion, the United States Supreme Court held that the provision of the Social Security Act that prohibited men from receiving social security benefits was unconstitutional. Not only did winning this case allow

---

155   Hopkins, Julie M. *Towards a Feminist Christology: Jesus of Nazareth, European women, and the Christological Crisis.* Grand Rapids: Eerdmans Publishing, 1994: 91
156   *Weinberger v Wiesenfeld* 420 US 636 (1975)

men like Mr. Wiesenfeld to collect on a deceased wife's social security benefits, it also gave a nod to men staying home with young children to care for their needs, and it helped legitimize women paying into the social security system.

When the gender equality cases were making their way through the United States Supreme Court, all nine justices were men. Being men didn't prevent them from becoming women's liberators through their opinions on gender equality cases. Jesus' maleness didn't prevent Him from being a women's liberator, it made Him the perfect one.

The Women in Jesus' Life and Ministry

In the story of the widow of Nain, Jesus heard the cries of a grieving and desperate woman.[157] The woman was a widow and her only son had just died. You can imagine the heart-break and the heart-wrenching sobs that were coming from the grieving mother. Jesus heard those cries and immediately responded with compassion. Jesus brought the son back to life for this woman, and in so doing restored the dignity and life of a woman, a mother. Had Jesus not raised her son from the dead, this widow, who was already poor, would have had no means of support and no hope for the future – she would have been pitied, shamed, and subjected to harsh treatment by society. Jesus, in this story, didn't make a public declaration that He was being a liberator; instead, He took action to save her from a life of oppression.

---

157   Luke 7:11-15

Jesus liberated women to work and provide. There were a number of women who followed Jesus during His ministry. These same women who previously were not allowed to read or study Scriptures followed Jesus, listened, and learned from Him and were referred to as disciples.[158] These women left families to travel from place to place, living as those in poverty, and supporting Jesus and His followers from their *own* resources. Interestingly, the Synoptic Gospels

> use the form of the verb *diakoneo* (to minister or serve) to describe what these women did in addition to saying that they 'followed' Yeshua. It is the same basic word as 'deacon'; indeed, apparently the tasks of the deacons in early Christianity were much the same as those these women undertook.[159]

It is the same word found in the Gospel, "For even the Son of Man came not to be served but to serve, and to give his life as a ransom for many."[160] It is the same word Paul used in Romans 15:25, "but now, I am going to Jerusalem serving the saints." Paul also used the word in 2 Corinthians 8:19-20 referencing himself and his own work. The use of the same verb indicates these women's service was the same as the men's, including Paul.

Jesus has not said that women can be ministers or deacons, but the fact that women followed Him and learned from Him during a time when those activities would have been

---

158 Swidler, 23.
159 Swidler, 74.
160 Mark 10:45 (NKJV)

prohibited and/or scandalous is Jesus' affirmation that women can and should take active roles in ministry. Furthermore, God doesn't show favoritism between men and women. Luke wrote in Acts 10:34-35, "So Peter opened his mouth and said: 'Truly I understand that God shows no partiality, but in every nation anyone who fears him and does what is right is acceptable to him.'" Jesus discussed theology with the woman at the well and stated Mary had chosen correctly by sitting and learning from Him. He didn't ignore women or their brains, and most importantly, He didn't ignore a woman's desire to pursue God.

Jesus liberated women to bear witness, to evangelize, to disciple, and to deliver the most important message ever given. Women in Jesus' day were not allowed to bear witness, or to give testimony; they were not considered trustworthy. Jesus turned that on its head. He first appeared to women after His resurrection, "a dramatic linking of a very definite rejection of the second-class status of women with the central element of the Gospel – the resurrection."[161] The very people who were not allowed to give testimony were the people He first appeared to as the Risen Christ. It was women to whom Jesus revealed Himself as the Messiah: to Martha "as the 'resurrection,' and to Mary Magdalene as the 'risen one'."[162] He went a step further with Magdalene and told her to go tell the other disciples, thereby entrusting in a woman the very thing that differentiates Christianity from other religions and is a core tenet of the faith. The most important thing to Christians

---

161   Swidler, 23.
162   Swidler, 27.

— Christ resurrected — was first entrusted in a woman to tell others. I mean, what more evidence could we need? The most important message, the essential message, the most glorious message was given first to a woman to tell. If Jesus trusted women enough to tell them first of His resurrection and then to command those women to go tell the men about the resurrection, who are we, mere humans, to say women can't be entrusted with God's Word and relaying His Word to men?

Jesus' revelation to the Samaritan woman that He was the Messiah resulted in this woman telling her village (i.e., "bearing witness") that Jesus is the Messiah, a core tenet of the faith. This woman became an evangelist. Jesus is releasing women from the belief that they are not reliable or trustworthy, that they cannot be ministers or bearers of the Good News. Jesus even took that a step further and commanded Mary Magdalene to "go and tell."

Jesus liberated women in regards to divorce. Jesus rejected polygamy, saying that two shall become one[163] and rejected the ability for men to divorce a woman for any reason. He was unequivocal that anyone who divorces for any reason other than sexual immorality commits adultery if they remarry.[164] This is liberating to women because the law allowed men to divorce women for any reason, leaving them destitute, poor, and outcast with no means of support. Jesus also stated that it was a sin for a husband to commit adultery against his wife

---

163   Matthew 19:5, Mark 10:8
164   Swidler, 29.

– a departure from the law recognized at that time that only married women could be guilty of committing adultery.[165] This was revolutionary in the fight for equality for women. We may still grapple with the issue of divorce and whether or not Christians should divorce, but here, Jesus levels the playing field for women. He then goes a step further to condemn men who commit adultery, again leveling the playing field. He is advocating for gender equality here, ensuring men and women both, equally, are held personally responsible for their offense.

Jesus liberated women from their only societal value as ones who give birth. As was mentioned earlier, when a woman said to Jesus "Blessed is the womb that bore you, and the breasts at which you nursed!" He replied, "Blessed rather are those who hear the word of God and keep it!"[166] Instead of confirming the stereotype of His mother as a mere incubator and milk bottle, Jesus affirmed her status as God's servant, as the young woman who boldly, faithfully stated, "I am the servant of the Lord; let it be to me according to your word," thus demonstrating to all the incredible faith and fortitude for which women are capable.[167] He affirmed God's calling on His mother's life – to literally give birth to the Good News.

Gender Roles

Gender has defined our roles in society throughout the centuries, defining the societal expectations of men and women.

165 Swidler, 57.
166 Luke 11:27-28
167 Luke 1:38

These roles are predominantly social constructs that have favored men and kept women in an oppressed state.[168] During Jesus' time on earth, wealthy women or women married to high ranking officials had much more freedom to engage in activities normally reserved for men, and of course were not worried about everyday concerns such as food and shelter. However, the majority of women were not educated and worked mostly in the home and raising children.

For Jesus' part, He favored a woman getting an education over doing housework and serving food. In the story of Mary and Martha, Martha assumes the typical gender role of cooking and serving household guests whereas Mary sits at Jesus' feet to listen to Him.[169] The practice of sitting at a teacher's feet was traditionally reserved for men. Mary took on the male role of listening to a teacher, learning, and in all respects assuming the role of a disciple of a rabbi/teacher. Jesus declared that Mary had chosen what is better. Jesus is saying here, "Let women learn," over the traditional woman's role and expectation of serving guests. Swidler wrote of this liberating discourse:

> When one recalls the Palestinian restriction on women studying the Scriptures or studying with rabbis, that is, engaging in the intellectual life or acquiring any 'religious authority,' it is difficult to imagine how Yeshua could possibly have been clearer in his insistence that

---

168   Dube, 353.
169   Luke 10:38-42

women were called to the intellectual, the spiritual life just as were men.[170]

Jesus further broke those gender roles when He commissioned Mary Magdalene and the other women at the tomb to go tell the disciples that He had arisen. She obeyed and was the first person to preach the Gospel to others; in other words, she evangelized. I love one of Merriam-Webster's definitions of evangelist, "an enthusiastic advocate".[171] Can't you just imagine Mary Magdalene's enthusiasm when running to tell the men about Christ's resurrection? Jesus gave permission to this woman to tell the Good News, to break free from the man-made structures that oppressed, silenced, and marginalized her and other women. Don't overlook a major point that Jesus made here: Jesus said, "but go to My brothers and say to them, I am ascending...."[172] He said "go", He _sent_ Mary Magdalene to deliver the message of the Good News to _men_. Jesus didn't tell her to go tell "the women", He told her to go and tell His "brethren."

Liberation

African feminist theologian Musa Dube rightly asked, "Who do you say I am?" She then writes that church traditions have for centuries named Christ for us, giving us (women) a Christology.[173] Christology is simply the study of Christ.

---

170 Swidler, 31.
171 "Evangelist." https://www.merriam-webster.com/dictionary/evangelist accessed January 23, 2021.
172 John 20:17
173 Dube, 346.

Simpler put, it was men telling women the how and what to think of Christ and His life as applied to women. However, it is now time for women to name Christ for ourselves.[174] How is that done for women? Liberation theologians state:

> the experience out of which Christian theology has emerged is not universal experience but the experience of the dominant culture.... Recognizing inherent problems in the universalist approach to the doing of theology... theology must emerge out of particular experiences of the oppressed people.[175]

Grant goes on to write, "Since experience is the context in which Christological interpretation takes place, before women begin to reflect on Jesus Christ, they must claim the power to name themselves and their experience so that their Christological reflections would be authentically theirs."[176] We need more women in theology and more in denomination and church leadership to accomplish this. These scholars confirm what we all know and what I wrote earlier in this book: men and women are different, and we experience Christ differently.

We need to see scholarship, books, and sermons that reflect our unique view and experience with Jesus. Women need to be part of the decision-making in churches on more than just children's ministry and music. Women need to be part of doctrinal and theological discussions and decisions. When allegations of

---

174 Dube, 347.
175 Grant, 10.
176 Grant, 11.

sexual misconduct are made against a church leader, women need to be part of the investigation and response.

The experiences of women cover a broad spectrum. Developing a feminist Christological perspective in all aspects of women's lives, however, is as simple as looking to Jesus and studying every aspect of His life on earth. Jesus is the very heart of the Christian faith. All theology must start with Him. Everything starts with Jesus: from the pronouncement to Mary that she would give birth to Him to the last time we hear or see Him in Scripture. Paul's writings are part of the Bible, and they are important, but Paul isn't Jesus. What did Jesus say and do? How did He act and what did He not do? Ladies, we have to read and study the Bible and closely look at everything about Jesus' life.

Furthermore, liberation cannot wait. Jesus declared, "Today this Scripture has been fulfilled in your hearing."[177] Jesus declared in this statement and by His words and actions during His ministry that the exploitation — both political and economic — of the oppressed must stop; that today, freedom comes to those with no power and no voice and to those whom society has oppressed because of their gender, race, disability, or ethnicity.[178] "So if the Son sets you free, you will be free indeed."[179]

Conservative and evangelical women — at least this one writing this book — have been crying out for more

---

177   Luke 4:21; Dube, 348.
178   Dube, 348.
179   John 8:36

representation and freedom. To not respond to "women's cry for help is to deny their creation in God's image and to ignore their struggle for liberation."[180] We need to be loosed! Liberation for women, however, must come in different forms. Most women are too busy struggling against actual oppression to engage in academia about Jesus, God, the Trinity, or if the stories about Jesus helping women were merely stories to perpetuate the belief that men are the heroes and women are the only ones needing saving. Hannah Bacon writes that Asian feminists don't talk about God in the abstract because such discussion doesn't offer any tools or resources to assist Asian women in their struggle against oppression.[181] The same is true for a Brazilian and Latin American feminist theologian who wrote, "when faced with the realities of hunger, disease, war, unemployment, and meaninglessness, thinking about the Trinity 'would appear to be superfluous, hardly worth spending time on.'"[182] The realities of everyday life for most women beg for a relevant Christology that is liberating in their daily circumstances.

What does Jesus mean to the single mom struggling to pay the bills, put food on the table, and be a hands-on parent? What does Jesus mean to the woman who is homeless because she left a physically abusive marriage and had no money or nowhere to go? What about the teenager who ran away from her sexually abusive father, only to land in the arms of a pimp,

---

180 Njoroge, 429.
181 Bacon, Hannah. *"Thinking* the Trinity as Resource For Feminist Theology Today?" *CrossCurrents* 62, no. 4 (2012): 444.
182 Ibid, 444.

whom she calls "Daddy," and who now has her advertised as "fresh meat" online for sex services? What does Jesus mean to the bright-eyed college freshman at the University of Alabama, pursuing God's call on her life to be an attorney?

Men don't understand these circumstances. When I teach classes about recognizing and helping sex trafficking victims or how to help sexual assault victims, if there are men in the room, I ask this question to the men: how many of you walk out of the big box store at night worried someone is going to grab you at knife- or gunpoint and rape you? I've never had a man raise his hand. When I then ask the same question to the women, every woman raises her hand. Women and men have different concerns, different issues, and different experiences, and how we experience Jesus is different.

The liberation theology of women, to be real and practical, must meet the needs of women everywhere and in every condition. There must be a personal approach, an approach like Jesus'. Jesus was compassionate to women, showed tremendous grace, but also showed great respect for our faith, brains, and feistiness (I'm looking at you, Syrophoenician mom![183]).

Jesus addressed the realities of women's everyday lives in different ways, but not in any lengthy dialogue expressing the need for equality or any of His "Oh, snap!" parables. Jesus in His human and divine forms liberated women from the cultural chains of silence. He commanded them to go tell about His resurrection and He entrusted them with the most critical

---

183   Mark 7:24-30

message: His deity and resurrection. Jesus liberated women from the reproductive and household chains when refusing to limit His mother's importance to her child-bearing abilities. Jesus liberated women from the sexual education and political chains when He refused to allow one woman to be shamed for a sexual sin while ignoring the sins of others. He resurrected a widow's only son, saving her from living as a penniless and destitute woman with no way to help herself, which would have been her destiny without her son. His healing of the woman who bled freed her from a lifetime of banishment from society and religious life. She is now clean and welcome to worship.

Jesus demonstrated throughout His ministry that women were to be treated as equals; He shattered the gender roles of His society and advocated for women's equality and justice. Jesus has met the definition of a feminist – not the negative connotations that many conservatives have of that word, but the basic definition of belief that men and women should have equal rights and opportunities.

Jesus would have us answer the oppressed woman's cry for help without delay and in real and practical ways, the ways in which He did. He would have women learn and study His Word, as He did with Mary. He would have women engage in theological discussions as He engaged in such with the woman at the well. He would have us praise women who obey God's call on their lives, as He did His own mother. It puzzles me why, with the example Jesus set, we focus on a verse or two that Paul wrote. Paul is not Jesus.

This is where the American conservative and evangelical church can learn from SCOTUS. The same reasons used to justify the unequal treatment of women in the workforce and everyday life in America, are some of the same reasons used by church leaders to deny women leadership and preaching positions. SCOTUS, a man-made institution, determined those reasons were not sufficient to deny women equal opportunities, equal pay, and exclusion from "We the People."

CHAPTER 9
CULTURE

*"The truth is that the two sexes are not fungible;
a community made up exclusively of one is different from a
community composed of both.... Yet a flavor, a distinct quality
is lost if either sex is excluded"*[184]

When I entered law school, I was full of myself, thinking I must be really smart to be in law school. No one in my family was an attorney. I had no experience around the law, the legal jargon, or the different ways in which lawyers analyze issues. However, I had arrived. With all of the accolades from family and friends about merely getting into law school, I had a high opinion of myself and my intelligence. And then, I met my classmates. I felt dumber than dumb. I constantly questioned how in the world I was in the midst of these great minds that had graduated top of their respective undergraduate programs from all over the United States, some from top tier schools.

---

184   *J.E.B.* 133

Not only did I learn that I wasn't as smart as I thought I was, but I also learned I didn't know a thing about studying law. It's nothing like undergraduate learning. There was a new way to think and write essays. In college, I was a political science major with a concentration in political theory and an English minor; I thought I knew about critical thinking and essay writing. Most of my college exams were essays, so I had a lot of practice at that. I was, once again, wrong. Writing a legal essay is far different from what I had ever done.

At the end of my first semester of law school, I was placed on academic probation. I was mortified and confused. I knew God told me to go to law school; I knew this was His plan for me, so I didn't understand why this had happened. I knew the material. I studied all the time. One of my professors was kind enough to really walk me through what I was doing wrong and how to correct it. I had to learn this new way of thinking and writing in order to survive in this whole new world I had stepped into.

I learned by the end of the second semester how to properly write a legal analysis and brought my grades up tremendously. While in law school, I was part of a church college group called Twentysomething. We met every Monday night and averaged about 150-200 people each time. After my second semester grades came in, a very dear friend stood up and, much to my embarrassment and delight, gave a praise to God for me getting off academic probation! The room laughed, gasped, and applauded all at the same time. It was a classic moment that was equal part praiseworthy and equal part shock that she had told the entire audience that I had been on academic probation. But it was a testimony that God is faithful. We have to do the work as well, but He is faithful to continue the work in you that He starts. I had been redeemed from possible expulsion for poor academic performance and restored to good standing with the law school. My determination to finish what God had started in me was redeemed as well.

That first year of law school is generally difficult as we adjust to a new way of thinking, studying, and writing. Law students are told to study at least two hours outside of class for every hour that we are in class. That's a lot of studying when you consider I was in class 15 hours per week! It was not unusual, particularly close to final exams, for me to be studying or in class from 5:00 am until 11:00 pm. I would spend all day in the law library at my little cubicle, in my jeans and fleece pullover because it was so cold regardless of the season, and socks with Birkenstocks. I could easily slip off my shoes, get comfortable, and nibble on my peanut M&Ms to get me through the long day of studying. When I left law school, I didn't think there would be room to cram anything else into my brain. It was full, or so I thought.

God got the last laugh though. He stirred in me the desire to get my Master of Divinity. Consequently, I applied at Regent University for their online graduate program. This would allow me to remain in Alabama and continue my legal practice, but take classes online, only traveling to campus a few times a year. When I applied and was accepted into the Master of Divinity program at Regent University, there was a lot I didn't know about studying the Bible. You would think it'd be pretty simple, right? Isn't it just reading Scripture? I quickly learned otherwise. There are words for studying Scripture that I had never heard. I had gone through law school and had been an attorney for over 10 years when I started at Regent. I knew the legal jargon and understood most of the Latin phrases that refuse to die in legal writings. I didn't think there'd be too many words in the English language I had never encountered. Imagine my surprise when I saw the name of a required class and thought, HermanWHO?

Hermeneutics

I had never in my life heard the word hermeneutics until I started registering for classes and saw that Hermeneutics was a required class. I had to google that word to even see what it meant. I was clueless.

Traditionally, hermeneutics is the science that sets forth the methods or principles for interpreting the Bible. Today, most scholars recognize it as the way to narrow or clarify a text's meaning for the present day rather than what it originally meant. That is, what does Scripture mean for us today? As I had with law school, I learned that I had entered a whole new world with a new language set. I thought, *Great, here we go again!!* My first encounter with a new lingo particular to a profession had ended in a semester on academic probation.

Thankfully, I did much better in my first semester at Divinity than I did in law school! As I did with legal terms, I had to learn how to understand and convey them in real person terms. For example, as a prosecutor, I was always reading police reports. Whenever there was a traffic stop involved, invariably the law enforcement officer would write that the suspect "exited the vehicle." We don't use "exited" in everyday language, so I'd have to instruct the officer and be careful myself to use everyday language with a jury. Instead of "exited" we always say "got out of" the vehicle. So, at trial, we would say "got out of." It doesn't sound as sophisticated, but the message is the same.

Hermeneutics sounds scary. It sounds like something that would be hard to do because it's hard to even say! But it's a hoity toity word for what we all do, on some level, when we study the Bible. Hermeneutics is about interpreting the Bible. As Christians, we all have the ability to read and interpret the Bible. My dad would say from the pulpit that you should never trust what a preacher tells you the Bible says; always read it for yourself and know what it says.

In fact, the task of interpreting the Bible for the professionals is the same as for each of us who read and study it on our own: (1) third-person approach: what does the Scripture mean (using exegesis, which is discussed below)? Then to (2) first-person approach: what does this mean for me? Then to (3) second-person approach: how do I share what this means?[185]

---

185 Osborne, Grant R. *The Hermeneutical Spiral: A Comprehensive Introduction to Biblical Interpretation.* Downer's Grove: Intervarsity Press, 1991: 21.

Professionals take it to a depth that we may not, but the principle is the same.

Hermeneutics takes us from Biblical text to real world context. This is an important concept when we read the Bible. We can't take one Scripture out of context. Grant Osborne, PhD, author of *The Hermeneutical Spiral: A Comprehensive Introduction to Biblical Interpretation* wrote:

> Hermeneutics is important because it enables one to move from text to context, to allow the God-inspired meaning of the Word to speak today with as fresh and dynamic a relevance as it had in its original setting... The basic evangelical fallacy of our generation is 'proof-texting,' that process whereby a person 'proves' a doctrine or practice merely by alluding to a text without considering its original inspired meaning.[186]

Exegesis

Another new word and concept I learned in my first semester at Regent was exegesis. Whereas hermeneutics was the science and the overall approach, exegesis focuses on the what, why, and intentionality behind what was said or written. What did the author mean when he wrote it? The why can include a look at the historical context – what was happening in that society at the time it was said or written. Preachers, when preparing for a sermon, use exegesis to form a basis and understanding of a Biblical text and then apply it to today's church and society.

---

186   Osborne, 22.

Cultural Context

The Bible, though inspired by God, was written by humans, with all of their personal biases and experiences, and within their cultural context. We can never lose sight of that. Within the Bible are texts that transcend culture – values to which all cultures, regardless of century, should adhere. We call these Kingdom values. They are values such as loving your neighbor, forgiving those who have sinned against you, feeding the hungry, clothing the naked, and caring for widows and orphans. Then, there are texts we call cultural values that do not transcend cultures and are not timeless.

Cultural values are important to know and understand when interpreting Scripture. Cultural values contain significant cultural components such as slavery, treatment of women, and treatment of the diseased (such as the bleeding woman whom Jesus healed). Though we don't necessarily like the IRS, we don't despise tax collectors as was common in Paul's day. An exploration of cultural values is a look at what was happening in the culture at the time of what was spoken or written. Does the text have application between cultures and over the generations? Is it a time-bound truth or is it a timeless truth?

The writers were writing within their cultural contexts and understanding, and within the writing styles for their time. There is nothing sacrilegious about recognizing the humanity of the authors of these sacred texts. God used each of the writers as they were, in the time in history in which they lived. We are not casting doubt on the Scriptures or their authority as God's Word. In fact, some of the things they wrote would have been considered progressive for their time. For example, in the New Testament, women followed Jesus, engaged with Him in theological discussions, bantered with Him about whether or not to heal a child, followed Him, listened and learned from Him, spread the Good News that Jesus was the awaited Messiah, spread the Good News that Jesus was resurrected, owned businesses, taught, and instructed men to go out into the ministry with Paul, and many others.

Slavery as a Cultural Value

Slavery existed at the time Paul lived and wrote his letters to Timothy and others. As we all know, slavery existed for centuries following and continues to this day. I need to note here, that the slavery in the Bible is different from the evil endured by the hundreds of thousands of slaves in America who were dehumanized and treated as property, not humans, until the passage of the 13th Amendment in 1865.[187] It is different than the slavery experienced by sex and labor trafficking victims in the present day. However, we now know that slavery, in whatever form, is an evil that we do not tolerate. The same Paul who wrote in 1 Timothy 2:12 that he didn't permit women to teach, a verse still clung to by conservative and evangelical Americans, is the same Paul who wrote in 1Timothy 6:1 (NKJV), "All who are under the yoke of slavery should consider their masters worthy of full respect...." Scripture that

---

187   Webb, 44.

136

seems to support slavery, including those written by Paul, have not stood the test of time.

In all my years working with sex trafficking victims, I would have never told one of those young women I talked to on the phone that they had to honor and respect their trafficker/master. If the scripture Paul wrote was indeed considered correct today, then to the young woman who believed it was a sin if she refused sex with the men her adopted dad brought home to rape her, because saying no meant she didn't "honor her father" as the Ten Commandments required, I would have said – "That's right", because Paul wrote you had to honor your master. Paul also wrote in Ephesians that slaves should be obedient to their masters, so I guess since we follow everything Paul wrote, the sex slaves of today should stay where they are and do what their masters say? Obeying everything Paul wrote, I would have told the young lady that I spoke to standing on the street corner to hurry up and find herself a john and earn her "daddy" some money off her body. To the young woman who was lying in the hospital bed following life-saving surgery from a brutal rape with an object from a john, I would have told her to hurry up and heal so that she could return to her trafficker and be internally mutilated again. I mean, she's got to obey and honor her master, right? Of course, we do not and will not say these things to slaves of any kind. It's ludicrous. We now know and believe slavery to be a sin. Subjecting another human to forced labor or sexual servitude is sinful, and as I've seen firsthand, I can tell you that it is pure evil.

The ancient culture was particularly harsh and cruel to women and the oppressed. It doesn't have to be cruel or harsh in 21st Century America. As a society, we've made significant advancements in how we treat one another, but we are not yet at the point we treat one another equally.

Legal Interpretation

Like the Bible, there are different ways to interpret the Constitution. In 2020, we had the opportunity to hear about this, given the highly charged Supreme Court appointment process of Justice Amy Coney Barrett.

The nomination to the United States Supreme Court of Amy Coney Barrett in September 2020 to replace the late Ruth Bader Ginsburg was controversial. Controversy about whether or not to even proceed with a nomination so close to the presidential election aside, it also highlighted other controversies about women, feminists, conservatives, and conservative Christianity.

The process highlighted the divide between conservative and liberal women. There was much made at the hearings by Senators and within news and social media about the "Notorious R.B.G." championing equality and suggesting Judge Barrett does not champion equality because she holds pro-life views. Equality is not limited to women of one political party or view on abortion. A woman can be conservative, hold pro-life views, and champion equality for women.

Justice Barrett's confirmation fight brought forth supporters from the conservative evangelical leaders, championing her and her nomination and confirmation. Ironically, these same leaders would be the very ones saying she could not preach in their church's pulpits. Some of the same people who want her on the highest court of the United States, making decisions that affect every aspect of American life, including religious liberties, would not want her to preach God's Word in a church or in any way lead the church, where men are included, simply because she's a woman. Does that make any sense?

The national attention over Justice Barrett's confirmation highlighted differences in interpretating the Constitution. The primary methods of interpretation are discussed below; however, the buzz was that she, as a Justice Scalia protégé, was an originalist and what that meant for how she would decide issues before the Court. There are parallels when interpreting the Bible and the Constitution. In both, we look to the context of when it was written, what the culture was like when it was written, and whether it's a value or right that transcends time and changes in culture or not. Sounds like exegesis, right? There are two styles of interpreting the Constitution that generate the most discussion and debate, namely static/originalist and redemptive/living interpretations.

Static and Living

A static interpretation is sometimes called a "dead" or "stationary" interpretation. This means that the document being interpreted died at the time it was written. It doesn't evolve with time; we interpret it based on what the original public meaning was at the time it was written. Originalists, such as the late Justice Antonin Scalia and current Justice Amy Coney Barrett, look at the meaning of words at the time of writing. They look to other writings and texts of the time, and what was said during debates about the law or Amendment by the legislators.

A living constitutionalist believes the Constitution adapts with time, adapting to changing culture – as social attitudes change, the meaning of the Constitution changes. Justice Ruth Bader Ginsburg was a living constitutionalist. She, Justice Thurgood Marshall, and others have often noted that the original Framers of the Constitution were property-owning (aka wealthy) white men, who did not reflect fully "We the People." Therefore, if the phrase "We the People" were to be interpreted using originalism, the Constitution would only apply to wealthy white men, and obviously that is not what we want for our country.

Both sides can reach the same or similar conclusion about issues, but the way in which they get to the answer is different. I remember in math class, I could get the right answer, but if I didn't show how I reached that answer, and if the how didn't match the way I was taught, points were deducted from my answer. It was frustrating. The overall answer was correct, I just used a different method.

Similarly, those interpreting the Constitution can reach the same conclusion on an overall issue, but use different methods to get there. For example, both sides can agree that racial segregation is wrong. Originalists will say it's bad and wrong, always has been and always will be, because the 14th Amendment declares it so. Living constitutionalists say it's wrong because the social attitudes and public opinion through the years shifted and it is now disfavored.

The idea of originalism tends to be favored more by conservatives because the idea of a law evolving is not pleasant to our sensibilities. The same is true for Scripture. We believe Scripture is infallible. Though Scripture may be infallible, our interpretation of Scripture is certainly not. We have confused the two and, to preserve the order and hierarchy, we've meshed the two and believe that our interpretation and resulting doctrines are infallible. And, as Christians, we don't want our doctrine evolving. Heck, we don't even like the word evolution.

Indeed, it is hard to think of the Bible evolving. We can't alter the Bible or the Words of God. We can't change the things Jesus said or that Paul wrote. The Word of God is the Word of God! The Bible, like the Constitution of the United States, needs to be constant, a steady force in the chaos of this world. They need to be the cornerstone. The stability of an entire structure is determined by this stone. The Bible is the cornerstone for Christians and the Constitution is the cornerstone for Americans. We need them strong and sturdy.

Conversely, we need both the Constitution and the Bible to evolve over time. So much has changed over time that both have had to adapt to some of those changes. If either the Bible or the Constitution didn't change, but rather remained unmovable, both would be considered relics that could no longer fit in society, and thus have no relevancy to our lives. Changes such as slavery, international relations, racial equality, gender equality, family dynamics, and technological advances have all required some movement in how the Constitution and the Bible are interpreted.

The doctrine of our churches has been afforded the air of infallibility. We trust that the men who are deciding on doctrine are seeking God and for the Holy Spirit to guide and direct them on how and what to do with issues that face the church. But, as with Scripture and the Constitution, the men deciding doctrine come with biases, personal experiences, and cultural contexts. Some of the biases and cultural contexts include power and the desire to maintain power.

As with the Bible, the words of the Constitution and its Amendments are established, and the words do not evolve. But the meaning that we ascribe it does when presented with challenges to its application in real life. The Constitution, like the Bible, was written by men with all their biases and personal experiences. We say that we live in a Christian nation and that our nation was founded on Christian principles. If we believe that, and if we believe in the power of the Supreme Court to ensure those Christian principles are upheld, it would be hypocrisy to deny the principles of equality that SCOTUS has routinely declared as foundational principles for this country.

Lessons Learned from SCOTUS

The *Frontiero* court made clear that merely being female does not impose a special disability upon us. Imposing a "special disability" on the members of a particular sex because of their sex violates the basic concept within our legal system that there be some relationship to individual responsibility when denied an opportunity. The same is true for a Christ follower. Who is man to impose a special disability upon women who have an individual responsibility to God? God doesn't impose a special disability on women when it comes to spiritual gifts. God gives us the gifts and we have the individual responsibility to use those gifts for the furtherance of His Kingdom. We know there will come a time when we will have an individual responsibility for what we did with the life God gave us. Christians believe there will be an accounting, a judgment, as to what we did with the gifts and talents God gave us to love His people and further His Kingdom.

Individual responsibility is a concept Christians should fully and completely understand and to which we should relate. We believe we are each responsible for our own salvation. When we stand before God, there is no one else responsible for our salvation but us. Whether or not I accepted Jesus as my Lord and Savior is based on my decision, my choice.

Furthermore, what I did with my God-given talents, abilities, and my spiritual gifts is my individual responsibility. I alone will be judged on that when I get to heaven. Just as the servants in the parable of the five talents, I am responsible for investing and growing what God has given me.[188] In the story of the five talents, a master gives his servants/workers money in different amounts to take care of while he's gone. Two of the three servants increase the amount they were initially given but the third hides the money so that it won't be stolen. When the master returns from his trip, he asks each of the three men what happened with the money he gave them. Each one of those men has to answer his boss. The servants in that parable answer to their master individually. The servant with the five talents doesn't give an answer for the servant with the one talent. The servant with the five talents isn't accountable for the servant with the one talent. I, not anyone else, will be held accountable to God for how I used the talents and abilities God gave me.

"The accident of my birth," being a female, should not keep me from fully functioning in the gifts and talents God gave me. Whether the gifting is wisdom, teaching, administration, prophesying, healing, or any of the other enumerated spiritual gifts, the spiritual gifts are given to each person, regardless of their gender.[189] And, regardless of my gender, God will ask me what I did with the gifts He gave me. If my spiritual gift is teaching or preaching, God will hold me accountable for how I used what He gave me. I don't think I can get away with saying, "Well, God, you see, my denomination said I couldn't teach because, even though You gave me the gift of preaching, You accidentally made me a woman with those gifts. Sorry!"

---

188   Matthew 25:14-30
189   Romans 12:6-8, Ephesians 4:7-12, 1 Corinthians 12

Ms. Reed was not disqualified from handling her son's estate because she did not have the ability to do all that was necessary to administer an estate. She had the gifts and talents to be able to accomplish what was needed. Lt. Frontiero was not disqualified from receiving the spousal benefits because she could not perform her duties in the United States Air Force. She was qualified in her role and had all of the gifts, talents, training, experience, and ability to perform her job honorably. Where these two women "fell short" was their immutable characteristic of womanhood. The United States Supreme Court said that wasn't sufficient reason. A man-made institution that is revered by Christians across America, in which conservative Christians have placed their hope, trust, and faith, has declared that mere womanhood cannot prevent women from being treated equally. "If you then, who are evil, know how to give good gifts to your children [read: women], how much more will your Father who is in heaven give good things to those who ask Him?"[190] That is, if an imperfect group of men can determine that women shouldn't be denied equality due to the mere fact of being female, how much more will our perfect, loving, and just Father in heaven determine and do?

There has been a lot written and said about Paul's writings about women as preachers, leaders, and even speaking in church. Though I touch on some of those issues, this is not meant to be an in-depth analysis of Paul's writings on women in the church and the 1 Corinthians 11 issues. I encourage you

---

190   Matthew 7:11

to research Paul's writings, but be sure to read all of what he wrote, and keep in mind he is not Jesus.

Paul's declaration in Timothy, "I do not permit a woman to teach or to exercise authority over a man; rather she is to remain silent," is comparable to a legislative body passing a statute or law. Statutes created by Congress or a state's legislative body have to pass constitutional muster.[191] They cannot violate anyone's rights guaranteed by the Constitution, America's cornerstone. Similarly, what Paul wrote has to be compared to the words and actions of Jesus —Christians' cornerstone. What is it that Jesus tells us and teaches us? What Paul wrote is from him, it's not a command from God. Jesus never said anything about not permitting women to do anything. Paul wrote, "I do not permit..." – "I" meaning him, Paul, the apostle who came from the steeped patriarchal tradition and in a Roman society that did not permit women to teach. Interestingly, the men who spent every day with Jesus during His ministry on earth, didn't place any prohibitions on women in their writings. It seems to me that if Jesus had a problem with women in leadership or preaching, the ones who knew Him best, and literally saw Him interact with women daily, would have addressed it. To be clear, Paul wasn't one of those men.

His explanation for this in the next verse is that God created man first, so based on the order of creation, women should not be leaders or teachers over men. Paul's explanation falls within the "immutable characteristic" that was addressed

---

191   1 Timothy 2:12

by the U.S. Supreme Court. How much more immutable can you get than the beginning of creation when God created heaven and earth, man and woman?

We've already debunked the hierarchical argument because Jesus came and leveled the playing field. To look back at the creation story though, God said, "Let us make man in our image...".[192] God said "Our" meaning Father, Son, and Holy Spirit, what we call the Holy Trinity. Just as in the Trinity, One is not greater than the other, similarly, we humans who are created in _Their_ image are equal, one with another.

What are we doing to young women who have the desire, the talent, the ability, and more importantly the call to preach? We have told them it's acceptable to preach to other women but it's not okay to preach to men. If God has called Beth Moore to preach in her church where men are present, she is the one who has to answer to God if she doesn't follow that call. In conservative churches, we have created a "separate but equal" segregation of the sexes. However, the premise that there be separate but equal teachers for women and men, as well as for events, is a concept previously denounced by SCOTUS in rulings on secular issues.

As Christians, we believe that God's laws are higher than man's laws. So, if man can recognize that women cannot be treated differently merely because they are women, why do we believe anything less of God? Why do we ignore it when God has a woman leader in Israel, Deborah, who is also a military

---

192   Genesis 1:26

leader going into battle? Why do we ignore that Jesus talked theology with the woman at the well? Why do we ignore that the first people to whom Jesus appeared on that third day were women whom He would command to go and tell? And in fact, in the story where a woman was busying herself with "woman's work" — cooking and cleaning — Jesus said that she had not chosen wisely, she should rather have been listening and learning.[193]

---

193   Luke 10:42

CHAPTER 10
THE COURAGE TO BE DEFIANT
TO MAN BUT OBEDIENT TO GOD

'Who's the people that really keeps things going on? It's women. The women is the ones that supports the deacon board. They holler the amen. The women is the ones that supports the preacher.... So in the black community the movement quite naturally emerged out of all the women that carried out these roles. We didn't know we was leaders. You knew you did things, but you never saw it as a high political leadership role.' [194]

We the People... to form a more perfect union.... Equality demands justice and righteousness. In our recent history, we've seen the linking of equality with justice in an actionable form. The Civil Rights Movement of the 1950s and 1960s firmly linked the two concepts, providing us an example of these concepts in action. The prophets of the Old Testament

---

[194] Olson, Lynne. *Freedom's Daughters.* New York: Touchstone. 2001, 251. Quoting Unita Blackwell, former Mississippi sharecropper, leader of Mississippi Civil Rights movement, and first African-American female elected mayor of a Mississippi municipality.

were often quoted by those seeking justice. Martin Luther King, Jr. invoked Amos when he gave his "I Have a Dream Speech" saying, "we will not be satisfied until justice rolls down like waters, and righteousness like a mighty stream."[195]

Women and Black Americans have a shared history in America of oppression. I do not at all suggest the shared oppression is equal. The oppression of people of color in this country has been cloaked in hate and evil the likes of which white women, generally, haven't seen or experienced. But, there's a shared struggle in fighting for equality in this country, and it starts with justice.

The concept of justice is woven throughout the Bible and Jesus' ministry while on earth. Micah tells us that the Lord requires us to "do justice, and to love kindness, and to walk humbly with [our] God."[196] In Isaiah 1:17, the prophet wrote, "learn to do good; seek justice; correct oppression; bring justice to the fatherless, plead the widow's cause." The prophets were very clear about the importance of justice. Isaiah, in chapter 28, wrote about the "cornerstone", that is Jesus, being laid in Zion and He — Jesus — is a sure foundation such that the person who believes in Him will be unshakable. Isaiah then wrote, as a direct message from God, "And I will make justice the measuring line and righteousness the mason's level."[197]

---

195   Amos 5:24
196   Micah 6:8
197   Isaiah 28:16-17

Righteousness and Justice

The terms "righteousness" and "justice" are often used together and at times interchanged throughout Scripture. The righteousness/justice word duo, found in the Hebrew Bible some 30 times, is used throughout Judaic history in various ways often intertwined with words such as "truth" and "kindness."[198] The definition of the term has evolved and its use is fluid. Righteousness can refer to, for example, a legal concept, such as a judicial proceeding, or the covenant between God and man, or to social justice. To some scholars, its usage can be summed up in one all-encompassing concept: salvation.

Some of the common beliefs held as Christ-followers, are to provide for the needy, protect the weak, and help those who are oppressed. Those principles date back to the patriarchal period, where "justice and righteousness" are first seen as a word pair wherein Abraham and his descendants are charged with *doing* righteousness and justice.[199] These teachings form the basis for the use of righteousness and justice within the social context, that is, to *perform* acts of righteousness and justice. The idea of helping the poor, hungry, widowed, and others within the lower spectrum of society was seen earlier in Jewish society; for example, Ezekiel and Isaiah wrote that providing food and clothing to the poor is required.[200] It was

---

198 Marlon, Hilary. "Justice for Whom? Social and Environmental Ethics and the Hebrew Prophets" in *Ethical and Unethical in the Old Testament: God and Humans in Dialogue*. ed. by Katharine Dell. New York: T&T Clark International, 2010: 104.
199 Ibid 104.
200 Weinfeld, Moshe. *Social Justice in Ancient Israel and in the Ancient Near East*. Minneapolis: Fortress Press, 1995: 222.

to these prophets that the Jews looked when faced with the unrest in their own society.

Righteousness is a "basic ethical demand for humans living together," a concept central to Jews and Christians.[201] The biblical use of the term "refers broadly to 'doing, being, declaring, or bringing about what is right.'"[202]

The linking of "justice" and "righteousness" and the interchange of the terms throughout Scripture are intentional. In the Old Testament, "what is just is intrinsically bound up with what is good... justice is ordered toward righteousness; in particular, it is directed toward the establishment of right relations between people and God."[203] Righteousness and justice are concerned with the deliverance and liberation of the oppressed, the poor, the destitute, and indeed of all of humanity. It is redemptive and salvific. It is the "'foundation' of God's throne, the fundamental ground of the cosmos."[204]

As we shall see below, there are exhortations to *do* justice; that is, to perform acts of kindness and charity and to treat others justly. However, first and foremost, the idea of righteousness and justice is an extension of God's design to deliver man from sin.[205] When the term righteousness is used outside of the legal concept, it is inherently a term associated with the sense of "right order, a situation that is according to God's

---

201 Henning Graf Reventlow and Yair Hoffma, eds. *Justice and Righteousness: Biblical Themes and their Influence*. Sheffield: JSOT Press,1992: 163.
202 Marshall, Chris. *The Little Book of Biblical Justice*. Intercourse: Good Books, 2005: 11.
203 Bell, Daniel M Jr. "Jesus, The Jews, and the Politics of God's Justice". *Ex Auditu* (2006): 87-112, 100.
204 Marshall, 23.
205 Bell, 100.

will, design, plan, way and ordination... a righteous action is one that either maintains or restores the right order."[206] God's righteousness is salvific; it's deliverance, a saving *action*. It is thus, initially, a vertical concept that requires action by God to deliver man. This then transcends to a horizontal concept for man to do what is just and right to his fellow man. Jesus was the embodiment of restoring right order, both vertically and horizontally, of righteousness and justice.

Social Justice

Equal protection under God has perhaps no more important piece than social justice. To the prophet Isaiah, justice and righteousness are about action: "to loose the bonds of wickedness, to undo the straps of the yoke, to let the oppressed go free, and to break every yoke... to share your bread with the hungry and bring the homeless poor into your house; when you see the naked, to cover him...."[207]

Reading the Bible, particularly the prophets, it is evident the authors believed the demand for social justice was directly from God, "who has determine[d] to secure the good and beneficial order of creation."[208] The establishment of justice begins with God. In the Old Testament, the order for just actions was from God to the king and then to all of the people. When the Jewish people no longer had a king, it became a horizontal

---

206 Campbell, John. "The Righteousness of God." *Affirmation* (September 2013): 80.
207 Weinfeld, 18; Isaiah 58:6.
208 "Righteousness Language in the Hebrew Scriptures and Early Judaism." *Justification and Variegated Nomism: The Complexities of Second Temple Judaism.* Vol. 1, ed. by D. A. Carson, Mark A. Seifrid, and Peter T. O'Brien. Tubingen: Mohr Siebeck; Grand Rapids: Baker Academic, 2001: 426.

relationship, such that men and women had to treat one another justly and care for one another. Individual responsibility to treat others justly and equally is substantiated by Jesus in Matthew 25:31-46 calling "blessed" those who performed acts to help those in need. We the people are to do justice to one another.

The terminology found in the Hebrew Bible further substantiates the expectation of action associated with this phrase. "To do righteous" [deeds, acts, etc.] occurs 24 times; "righteousness and just judgment" occurs 26 times, while "to judge righteously" occurs only 14 times and "righteous judgment" occurs only nine times.[209] This indicates the emphasis on action, on *doing*, not a mere concept or something abstract. Less judging, more action.

A source of conflict within the Judean society was that the ruling priestly aristocracy compromised their traditions, that is, their religion, to placate the Romans and keep their positions within society. They wanted the power; much like within new movements of the Holy Spirit, the organization of a new denomination ushers in positions of power and authority and certain people want to cling to the power.

Jesus told His disciples, when they were discussing who among them was the greatest, that whoever is the least will be the greatest.[210] Jesus later said to His disciples, "For who is the greater, one who reclines at table or one who serves? Is it not the one who reclines at table? But I am among you as the one

---

209   Seifrid, 428.
210   Luke 9:48

who serves."[211] Power and authority are not why Jesus gave His life. He told his disciples to "make disciples of all nations, baptizing them in the name of the Father and of the Son and of the Holy Spirit, teaching them to observe all that I have commanded you."[212] He didn't tell them, and consequently us, to exert power over others. When we get too big for our britches and God needs to get our attention to do what's right and act justly, He sends the women.

Strength of a Woman

While working on my Master of Divinity at Regent University, I stumbled upon the name of someone who would quickly become my hero. Civil rights activist Fannie Lou Hamer was the epitome of the black woman of the Civil Rights era – the "womanist": bold, daring, audacious, and outrageous."[213] While researching women of the Civil Rights movement of the 1950s and 1960s, I read about the incredible women engaged in the fight for racial equality.

The Civil Rights Movement was a hard-fought battle on the streets, in the church, and in the courts. Growing up in Alabama, I learned in school about Martin Luther King, Jr. and Rosa Parks, but that was about it – at least they're the only ones I really remember reading about. When at Regent and taking the class Women in Pentecostal History, I researched the women of the Civil Rights Movement. It was then that

---

211 Luke 22:27
212 Matthew 28:19-20
213 Hayes, Diana L. *Standing in the Shoes My Mother Made.* Minneapolis: Augsborg Fortress, 2011: 165.

I got a real education about that time in American history. Women I had never heard of before were suddenly my heroes in the faith and fight for equality. Fannie Lou Hamer and Diane Nash are just two of those women who subjected themselves to arrest, jail, beatings, name-calling, death threats, and much more in the struggle for Black Americans to realize the first words of the Constitution, "We the People... in Order to form a more perfect Union."

Fannie Lou Hamer

After hearing James Bevel of the Southern Christian Leadership Conference (SCLC) preach on August 27, 1962 from Luke 12:54, Fannie Lou Hamer, at the age of 44, responded and began her activism, equating the freedoms being sought by Blacks in America as being what the Lord required.[214] Hamer would soon have her faith and fortitude tested when she was arrested with others in Winona, Mississippi. Her reputation as an outspoken leader had preceded her and she endured the harshest beating of all of those arrested with her, suffering internal damage that remained with her until her death many years later. While in jail, however, she led the other women in singing "When Paul and Silas Were Bound in Jail," she repeated Bible verses that she thought would help her and the others remain calm and sustain them through the ordeal, and she even asked one of the jailers who participated in her beating, "[Did you] ever think or wonder how you'll feel when

214   Ross, 91.

the time comes you'll have to meet God?"[215] That's a good question isn't it?

After her severe beating in the Winona jail, she began speaking at events sponsored by the Student Non-Violent Coordinating Committee (SNCC). People were taken in by "her eloquence, her powerful singing, and her facility for coming up with colorful, ironic one-lines." [216] She was so effective, that Henry Kirksey, one of the first Blacks elected to the Mississippi Senate, declared "Fannie Lou had the ability to get the people worked up, much more so than Martin Luther King."[217]

Diane Nash

In the early 1960s in Nashville, Tennessee, college students united behind a young woman named Diane Nash. Nash began her fight against segregation and racism because she believed it to be a sin. For Nash, repentance from this sin of segregation was an urgent matter, and a change in behavior was just as urgent.[218] Nash stated that the nonviolent movement to end segregation is "applied religion…. I think it is the work of our church."[219] Nash's focus on redemption and loving like Christ loved invoked the image of Christ being crucified – on a cross. White supremacists have used the cross as a symbol of hate. James Cone in *The Cross and the Lynching*

---

215   Ross, 106.
216   Olson, 255.
217   Ibid.
218   Ross, 183.
219   Ross, 189.

Tree highlighted the contrasting use of the cross — the cross to Christ was a means by which to show His love for us; the cross to the KKK was a means to show hate — as the backdrop in comparing the lynching of Black Americans to the death of Christ on the cross.

Nash was urged into the student-led movement leadership by the men. She had become a strong and powerful voice, helped organize and participate in lunch counter sit-ins, and took over the organization of the Freedom Rides when others deemed it too dangerous. She was pressured by then Attorney General Robert Kennedy and the leaders of SCLC to call off the Freedom Rides due to the danger involved. Nash refused, hopped in a car, and drove to Birmingham, Alabama to pick up the riders who had been attacked in Anniston, Alabama, and accompanied them to their destination in Mississippi. She was the leader of the most successful student-led protests in the South and was regarded by many as the rightful leader of the newly formed student movement, SNCC. However, when SNCC held their first convention and elected its first set of officers, a male was voted as the leader. John Lewis, who would eventually become leader of SNCC, stated, "Diane was a devoted, beautiful leader but she was the wrong sex.... There was a desire to emphasize and showcase black manhood."[220]

These amazing women, and indeed many more from the Civil Rights Movement, applied their faith to fight for justice and equality. They were fighting for racial equality while being

---

220   Olson, 160.

denied gender equality. Yet, they followed the words of the prophet Isaiah to seek justice and correct the oppressor. These women had the ability to lead, but because of their immutable characteristic of womanhood, were denied leadership roles. The cause for racial equality was fought and won in the United States Supreme Court in cases such as *Brown v Board of Education* and *Boynton v Virginia.* The American conservative churches, at least in the South, rejected the call for racial equality, as noted by Martin Luther King, Jr.'s "Letter from a Birmingham Jail." They were on the wrong side of both history and God's command for justice. Perhaps the same is true for gender equality.

The Supreme Court helped pave the way for desegregation in churches. Redemption of the conservative and evangelical church, though, has not been achieved. There remains a deep hurt that has not healed and the wounds were ripped back open in the last few years. For women, the Supreme Court's rulings have not had a direct effect on women in leadership or preaching in the conservative and evangelical church; however, it has made clear the equality of women.

CHAPTER 11
REDEMPTION

"They were enslaved by law, emancipated by law, disenfranchised and segregated by law; and, finally, they have begun to win equality by law.[221]

A more perfect union. There is power in the word "redeem". Merriam-Webster defines redeem several ways:

1(a) to buy back (b) to get or win back; 2 to free from what distresses or harms: such as (a) to free from captivity by payment of ransom (b) to extricate from or help to overcome something detrimental (c) to release from blame or debt (d) to free from the consequences of sin; 3: to change for the better; 4: repair, restore; 5 (a): to free from a lien by payment of an amount secured thereby (b)(1) to remove the obligation of by payment (b)(2) to exchange for something of value (c)

---

221   Marshall, Thurgood. "The Constitution's Bicentennial: Commemorating the Wrong Document?" *Vanderbilt Law Review* 1337 (Nov 1987).

to make good; 6(a) to atone for (b)(1) to offset the bad effect of (b)(2) to make worthwhile.[222]

Forgive me for writing out the entire definition; each part of the definition describes what Jesus did for each of us when He died on the cross. Jesus' death was the price for buying us back, getting us back, payment of the lien against our lives for our sin, atonement for our sins, and making good on God's Word to save His people. Jesus' resurrection freed us from captivity, overcame our sin, released us from debt, freed us from the consequences of sin, and RESTORED us. That is power! Halleluiah! Amen!

But Jesus' redemption didn't end on the cross. Jesus redeems us still today. His redemptive power extends through the generations. God's Word is redemptive. There is redemption in the other words of Paul that declared there is "neither male nor female," in the subtle mention of Lydia as a home church leader, the praise of Mary for hearing God and obeying, and in Jesus' destruction of the hierarchical system. Jesus' love redeems. Jesus redeems. His words, His actions, the way He honored and valued women – whether it was His mother or a woman bleeding in the street reaching out to touch the hem of His garment. To believe these do not have redemptive power is to discount the resurrection.

American churches every year on or before July 4, celebrate this country and the Declaration of Independence that declared our independence from England. I've been in churches

---

222 "Redeem." https://www.merriam-webster.com/dictionary/redeem accessed November 23, 2020.

in which we put on patriotic programs, sang patriotic songs such as "God Bless America" and "America the Beautiful", and thanked God that we live in a society free to worship Him. Yet, we neglect to recognize that the Declaration of Independence declares, "all men are created equal, that they are endowed by their Creator with certain unalienable Rights...." We either believe those words written in 1776, plus those of the Constitution, its Amendments, and the jurisprudence of our revered United States Supreme Court apply to ALL people within the United States, or we're merely giving lip service to patriotism and love of country.

In the 1970s, women began to win equality through the law as SCOTUS rendered several opinions that women were to be treated equally, thus reinforcing the idea that "We the People" means all people, including women. Just as the Civil Rights Movement gained traction and victories in the court-rooms of America, so did the women. Almost 200 years after "We the People" was originally written, the United States Supreme Court repeatedly made it clear that "We the People" means everyone, regardless of race or gender.

Approximately 2000 years ago, Jesus liberated women, but the interpretation of Paul's words put us back in our cages. As a result, men have controlled doctrine, theology, purse strings, decisions over programs within the church, and what is preached from the pulpit on Sunday mornings. Capable and extraordinary women have been denied opportunities to lead and preach, due only to the fact they were women.

What message does this send to non-believers? The church is a reflection of God. The church is supposed to reflect God's love for His people and the world. For some, the rejection of women as capable of leading or preaching is a reflection of how God values — or doesn't — women. Even for believers, the rejection of women as leaders and preachers is repulsive and a stain on the church. It's difficult to reconcile the love of Christ, His respect and honor of women, and the conservative and evangelical church's treatment of women.

The Covid-19 pandemic has left many of us watching church services online rather than attending in person. As I watched online church recently, the pastor said he planned to do a series on values for the year 2021. He then said, "America has to return to its values."

The mixing of church with America and American values happens every Sunday in churches across this great nation. That's not necessarily a bad thing as long as there's a recognition that American values include equality and equal treatment of all of its citizens, regardless of race or gender. SCOTUS, an American institution and the pinnacle of the Judicial Branch of our government, has made it clear that equality is an American value and core principle. It is hypocrisy for the conservative and evangelical church to promote patriotism and nationalism but to reject the core principles of the Constitution of the United States, the equality of men and women of all races, the full meaning of those first three words, *"We the People."*

Ladies, you are the reason I wrote this book. God's love for you is immense. When I worked with victims of sex trafficking, a verse that God laid heavy on my heart was Jeremiah 31:3-4, "I have loved you with an everlasting love; therefore I have continued my faithfulness to you. Again I will build you, and you shall be built…". God will not start something in you that He won't finish. "And I am sure of this, that He who began a good work in you will bring it to completion at the day of Jesus Christ."[223] That's an amazing promise you can cling to. He's given you a message, a gift, and a purpose. He will build you, and rebuild when you're rejected on the basis of your sex.

You are loved, honored, and valued. You give value to the church and God's children, whether male or female. You are part of the body of Christ. Paul wrote,

> For as the body is one and has many members, but all the members of that one body, being many, are one body, so also is Christ… But now God has set the members, each one of them, in the body just as he pleased… And God has appointed these in the church: first apostles, second prophets, third teachers, after that miracles, then gifts of healings, helps, administration, varieties of tongues.[224]

As I read this verse and see "body of Christ", I see it as the Biblical equivalent to the Constitution's *"We the People."*

---

223   Philippians 1:6
224   1 Corinthians 12:12-14, 18, 28 (NKJV)

God does not discriminate based on our gender. He has given us gifts and abilities that only He can direct how they are used. He has placed us in a country full of opportunity and freedoms not realized by women in other countries. Though we struggle, we have victory in Him. Redemption for women and the church is found in Jesus alone, but an American institution has provided us a path. The Supreme Court of the United States has declared women give value to our country, deserve the opportunities afforded men in this country, and should be treated equally. Whether referencing the American Church or America itself, we women are truly a valuable, treasured, and equal part of *"We the People."*

BIBLIOGRAPHY

Alliaume, Karen Trimbe. "The Risks of Repeating Ourselves: Reading Feminist/Womanist Figures of Jesus". *CrossCurrents* 48, no. 2 (1998): 198-217.

Bacon, Hannah. "*Thinking* the Trinity as Resource For Feminist Theology Today?" *CrossCurrents* 62, no. 4 (2012): 442-464.

Bell, Daniel M. Jr. "Jesus, The Jews, and the Politics of God's Justice". *Ex Auditu* 22 (2006): 87-112.

Berquist, John. *Reclaiming Her Story: The Witness of Women in the Old Testament.* St. Louis: Chalice Press. 1992, 142.

Blue Letter Bible. https://www.blueletterbible.org/.

Boisnier, Alicia. "Race and Women's Identity Development: Distinguishing Between Feminism and Womanism Among Black and White Women." *Sex Roles* 49, nos. 5/6 September (2003): 211-218.

Campbell, John. "The Righteousness of God." *Affirmation* (September 2013): 78-92.

Clouse, Bonnidell and Robert Clouse, eds. *Women in Ministry: Four Views.* Downer's Grove: InterVarsity Press, 1989. Kindle.

Cohick, Lynn. *Women in the World of the Earliest Christians: Illuminating Ancient Ways of Life,* 190. Baker Academic, 2009. Kindle.

Cohick, Lynn, Amy Brown Hughes. *Christian Women in the Patristic World: Their Influence, Authority, and Legacy in the Second through Fifth Centuries.* Grand Rapids: Baker Academic, 2017.

DeFranza, Megan K. "The Transformation of Deception: Understanding the Portrait of Eve in the *Apocalypse of Abraham*, Chapter 23." *Priscilla Papers* 23, no. 2 (Spring 2009).

Dube, Musa W. "Who Do You Say That I Am?" *Feminist Theology*, 15.3 (2007): 346-367.

Duncan, Lauren E. "Women's Relationship to Feminism: Effects of Generation and Feminists Self-Labeling." *Psychology of Women Quarterly*, 34, no. 4 (2010): 498-507.

Fuchs, Esther. "Moses/Jesus/Women: Does The New Testament Offer a Feminist Message?" *CrossCurrents* (Winter 1999-2000): 463-474.

Fuchs, Lucy. *Women of Destiny.* Staten Island: Alba House, 2000.

Gench, Frances Taylor. *Back to the Well: Women's Encounters with Jesus in the Gospels.* Louisville: Westminster John Knox Press, 2004.

Ginsburg, Ruth Bader, Mary Hartnett, Wendy W. Williams. *My Own Words.* Read by Linda Lavin. Newark: Audible, 2016.

Grant, Jacquelyn. *White Women's Christ and Black Women's Jesus.* Atlanta: Scholars Press, 1989.

Grenz, Stanley. *Theology for the Community of God.* Grand Rapids, Eerdmans Publishing, 1994.

Hamilton, Victor P. *Handbook of the Pentateuch.* Second Edition. Grand Rapids: Baker Academics, 2005.

Hartley, John E. *Old Testament Survey: The Message, Form and Background of the Old Testament* Edition 2. Edited by William LaSor, David Hubbard and Frederick Bush. Grand Rapids, MI, 1996.

Hayes, Diana L. *Standing in the Shoes My Mother Made*. Minneapolis: Augsborg Fortress, 2011.

Henning Graf Reventlow and Yair Hoffma, eds. *Justice and Righteousness: Biblical Themes and their Influence*. Sheffield: JSOT Press, 1992.

Hopkins, Julie M. *Towards a Feminist Christology: Jesus of Nazareth, European women, and the Christological Crisis*. Grand Rapids: Eerdmans Publishing, 1994.

Ide, Arthur Frederick. *Battered & bruised: all the women of the Old Testament*. Las Colinas: Monument Press, 1993: 281.

Jackson, Glenna. "Jesus as First-Century Feminist: Christian Anti-Judaism?" *Feminist Theology: The Journal of the Britain & Ireland School of Feminist Theology*, 19 (September 1998).

King, Philip J. and Lawrence E. Stager. *Life in Biblical Israel*. Louisville: Westminster John Knox Press, 2001.

Konnikova, Maria. *The Confidence Game: Why we fall for it… every time*. New York, Penguin Books, 2017.

Machaffie, Barbara. *Her Story: Women in Christian Tradition*. Second Edition. Minneapolis: Augsburg Fortress, 2006. Kindle.

Marlon, Hilary. "Justice for Whom? Social and Environmental Ethics and the Hebrew Prophets" in *Ethical and Unethical in the Old Testament: God and Humans in Dialogue*. Edited byKatharine Dell. New York: T&T Clark International, 2010.

Marshall, Chris. *The Little Book of Biblical Justice*. Intercourse: Good Books, 2005.

Marshall, Thurgood. "The Constitution's Bicentennial: Commemorating the Wrong Document?" 40 *Vanderbilt Law Review* 1337, 1340 (Nov 1987).

Migliore, Daniel L. *Faith Seeking Understanding: An Introduction to Christian Theology*. Grand Rapids: Eerdmans Publishing, 2004.

Nelson Study Bible, The: New King James Version. Nashville: Thomas Nelson. 1997.

Njoroge, Nyambura. "Woman, Why are You Weeping?" *Ecumenical Review* 49 (1997): 427-438.

Osborne, Grant R. *The Hermeneutical Spiral: A Comprehensive Introduction to Biblical Interpretation*. Downer's Grove: Intervarsity Press, 1991.

Olson, Lynne. *Freedom's Daughters*. New York: Touchstone, 2001.

Penner, Todd and Lilian Cates. "Textually Violating Dinah: Literary readings, colonizing interpretations, and the pleasure of the text." *The Bible and Critical Theory* 3, no. 3 (2007).

Provan, Iain, V. Philips Long, and Tremper Longman III. *A Biblical History of Israel*. Louisville: Westminster John Knox Press, 2003.

Richards, Sue Poorman and Lawrence O. Richards. *Women of the Bible: The Life and Times of Every Woman in the Bible*. Nashville: Thomas Nelson, 2003.

Ross Rosetta E. *Witnessing & Testifying: Black Women, Religion, and Civil Rights*. Minneapolis: Ausburg Fortress, 2003.

Rouse, Carolyn Moxley. *Engaged Surrender: African American Women and Islam*. Berkeley: University of California Press, 2004.

Seifrid, Mark A. "Righteousness Language in the Hebrew Scriptures and Early Judaism." *Justification and Variegated Nomism: The Complexities of Second Temple Judaism*. Vol. 1,Edited By D. A. Carson, Mark A. Seifrid, and Peter T. O'Brien. Tubingen: Mohr Siebeck; Grand Rapids: Baker Academic, 2001: 415-42.

Swidler, Leonard J. *Jesus Was a Feminist: What the Gospels Reveal about His Revolutionary Perspective*. Lanham: Sheed & Ward, 2007.

Tucker, Ruth A. and Walter Liefeld. *Daughters of the Church*. Grand Rapids: Zondervan, 1987. Kindle.

Wainwright, Elaine M. *Shall We Look for Another?* Maryknoll: Orbis Books, 1998.

Weinfeld, Moshe. *Social Justice in Ancient Israel and in the Ancient Near East*. Minneapolis: Fortress Press, 1995.

Webb, William. *Slaves, Women & Homosexuals: Exploring the Hermeneutics of Cultural Analysis*. Downer's Grove: InterVarsity Press, 2001. Kindle.

Yee, Gale A. *Poor Banished Children of Eve*. Minneapolis: Augsburg Fortress, 2003.

Zlotnick, Helena. *Dinah's Daughters: Gender and Judaism from the Hebrew Bible to Late Antiquity*. Philadelphia: University of Pennsylvania Press, 2002.

TABLE OF CASES